TYPING and KEYBOARDING for EVERYONE

Nathan Levine

Sheryl Lindsell-Roberts, Editor

MACMILLAN • USA

Tenth Edition

Macmillan General Reference
A Simon & Schuster Macmillan Company
1633 Broadway
New York, NY 10019-6785

Copyright © 1996, 1994, 1992, 1989, 1985, 1980, 1978, 1976, 1974, 1971
by Nathan Levine

Library of Congress Cataloging-in-Publication Data

ISBN: 0-02-860597-7

Manufactured in the United States of America

1 2 3 4 5 6 7 8 9 10

TO THE BEGINNER

Typing for Everyone will teach you to type by touch—without looking at your fingers. These lessons "work." They were tested for ten years on 3,000 beginners, ages 14 to 70: students, clerks, cashiers, bookkeepers, salespeople, nurses, technical assistants, and workers in all sorts of jobs and occupations. All of them learned how to type quickly and expertly.

Type a lesson a day. Learn a few keys at a time; then as you practice words, sentences, and paragraphs, your control of those keys becomes automatic. Before you know it, you are a touch typist.

Here are some of the special features you will like about this book:

1. **Entirely Self-Teaching:**
   Each lesson is short, simple, and easy to master; it tells you plainly what to do and how to do it; it is your own private home tutor.

2. **Cumulative Review:**
   Beginning with Lesson 2, you review all the keys you have learned; you reinforce your control of those keys before you go on to the new ones. You can see your day-to-day progress toward your goal of typing mastery.

3. **Accuracy and Speed-Building in Same Lesson:**
   You get intensive accuracy and speed-building practice in the same lesson to develop your maximum typing skill. Interesting, flowing copy helps you reach specific goals.

4. **Word-Counted Material:**
   Sentences, paragraphs, and 1- to 5-minute copy tests tell you at a glance how many words you have typed in a given time.

5. **Timed-Typing Score Sheet:**
   A simple, easy-to-use score sheet for 1-, 2-, 3-, 4-, and 5-minute timed tests lets you see your day-to-day progress in speed-with-accuracy.

6. **Realistic Business Letter Placement:**
   No complicated scales to memorize. An all-purpose letter-placement formula tells you how to arrange quickly and attractively ALL styles of business letters.

7. **Simplified Tabulation:**
   No diagrams, no arithmetic. You learn the BACKSPACE way to type material in columns on a typewriter. If you are using a computer, check your user manual.

8. **Typing Aids:**
   Basic office "Know-Hows"—to help you become a proficient typist.

CONTENTS

PROGRESS CHART FOR TIMINGS

DATE	PAGE	WPM	ERRORS	DATE	PAGE	WPM	ERRORS

Correcting "Selectric" III

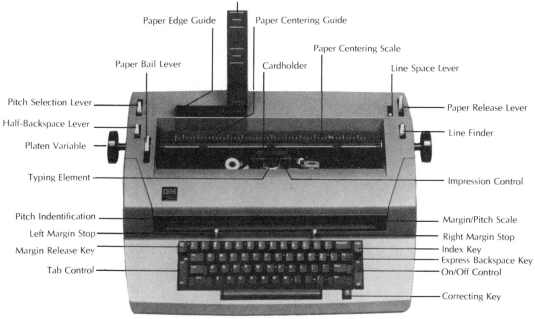

Page-End Indicator

Paper Edge Guide — Paper Centering Guide

Paper Bail Lever — Cardholder — Paper Centering Scale — Line Space Lever

Pitch Selection Lever — — Paper Release Lever

Half-Backspace Lever — — Line Finder

Platen Variable —

Typing Element — — Impression Control

Pitch Indentification — — Margin/Pitch Scale
Left Margin Stop — — Right Margin Stop
Margin Release Key — — Index Key
— Express Backspace Key
Tab Control — — On/Off Control

— Correcting Key

Computer Keyboard

The Backspace, Enter, and Shift keys are enlarged for convenience and located in their familiar Selectric positions.

The Escape key is isolated at the upper left of the keyboard to help reduce keying errors.

Dedicated function control keys are provided for frequently used functions such as Print Screen, Scroll Lock, and Pause.

The Tab and Caps Lock keys are enlarged and are located in their familiar Selectric positions.

Function keys are located across the top of the keyboard and spaced in groups of four. Two additional Function keys provide added flexibility in host access or communication applications.

The dedicated Numeric Pad includes its own Enter key and four Arithmetic Function keys, making it simple to work with numbers only.

Two Ctrl and Alt keys—one on each side of the space bar— offer easy access with either hand.

Screen Control and Cursor keys are separated from the numeric pad for easier, faster access.

Courtesy of IBM.

12. **Final F and FE**
    To Form the Plural:
    A. Add *s*: roof-roofs; chief-chiefs; giraffe-giraffes
       OR:
    B. Change the *f* to *v* and add *s* or *es*:
       life-lives; knife-knives; thief-thieves

13. **Final CE or SE?**
    When the noun and verb are similar:
    A. Write *ce* in nouns: advice, device, prophecy

    B. Write *se* in verbs: advise, devise, prophesy

14. **QU Combination**
    Always write *u* after *q*: acquit, banquet, question

15. **US or OUS?**
    A. Write *us* in nouns: callus, fungus, phosphorus

    B. Write *ous* in adjectives: callous, serious, tedious

16. **ABLE or IBLE?**
    A. Write *able* if you can form a word ending in *ation*:
       durable-duration; irritable-irritation

    B. Write *ible* if you can form a word ending in *ion, tion,* or *ive*:
       accessible-accession; collectible-collection; digestible-digestive

17. **CEED, CEDE, or SEDE?**
    CEED is only in: exceed, proceed, succeed
    SEDE is only in: supersede
    CEDE is in all other words: concede, intercede, precede,
                                 recede, secede

18. **Plural of Nouns**
    A. In most nouns, form the plural by adding *s*:
       house-houses; teacher-teachers

    B. In nouns ending in *s, sh, ch,* and *x,* add *es*:
       bus-busses; brush-brushes; watch-watches; box-boxes

19. **Plural of Compound Nouns**
    A. If the noun consists of one word, add *s*:   cupful-cupfuls
                                                      spoonful-spoonfuls

    B. If the noun consists of more than one word, add *s* to the principal word:
       mother-in-law   editor-in-chief
       mothers-in-law   editors-in-chief

20. **Prefixes and Suffixes Ending in ll**
    Omit one *l* in joining to other words: all-altogether
                                                full-wonderful

COMPUTER TERMINOLOGY

Alphanumeric	A combination of alphabetic and numeric characters.
Batch	A collection of similar work that can be produced in a single operation.
Bit	The smallest unit of information.
Buffer	The device in the computer that compensates for the rate of data flow.
Byte	A sequence of bits, usually shorter than a word.
CD	Compact disc that holds large amounts of information.
Character	A letter, number, symbol, or space.
Command	Instructions to the equipment to perform a certain function.
CPS	Characters per second (speed of typing).
CPU	Central processing unit (memory in a computer).
Crash	To become inoperable
CRT	Cathode ray tube (a television-like screen for the display of characters).
Cursor	The movable indicator on a CRT that indicates the place for editing a document.
Database or Data Base	Files of information used by an organization.
DBM	Database management, software used to center, organize, store, and retrieve data.
Debug	To locate and remove errors.
Delete	To remove a character, word, line, etc.
Disk (Diskette)	Equipment for the computer that is used for the recording, transcribing, and storage of data.
Dot Matrix Printer	A printer on which dots are arranged to form characters and graphic illustrations.
Down Time	Equipment inoperable.
Edit	To revise text.
Element	The removable, replaceable printing device resembling a ball.
Facsimile (FAX)	The transmission and reception of textual copy through telephone lines.

B. Drop the final *e* before a suffix beginning with a vowel:
    admire-admirable; desire-desirable; please-pleasure
    EXCEPTIONS: notice-noticeable; change-changeable
                   dye-dyeing; singe-singeing

5. **Final C**
Add *k* before joining to *ed, er, ing,* or *y:*
    picnic-picnicked-picnicker-picnicking
    panic-panicky

6. **Final CE**
Write the *e* before *able:*   peace-peaceable
                             service-serviceable

7. **Final GE**
Write the *e* before *ous:*   courage-courageous
                            outrage-outrageous

8. **Final OE**
Write the *e* before a suffix beginning with any vowel except *e:*
    hoe-hoeing-hoed
    toe-toeing-toed

9. **Final N**
Write the *n* before *ness:*   mean-meanness
                           sudden-suddenness

10. **Final O**
To Form the Plural:
A. If the *o* is after a vowel, add *s:*   cameo-cameos
                                     radio-radios

B. If the *o* is after a consonant, add *s* or *es:*   piano-pianos
                                                tomato-tomatoes

11. **Final Y**
To Form the Plural:
A. If the *y* is after a vowel, add *s:*   railway-railways
                                  attorney-attorneys

B. If the *y* is after a consonant, change *y* to *i* and add *es:*
    vacancy-vacancies
    country-countries

    NOTE: Write the *y* before *ing:*   testify-testifying
                                              accompany-accompanying

Field	A group of characters related for a specific purpose, somewhat like a column.
Floppy Disk	A disk used to store and retrieve programs and data.
Font	An assortment of characters in a certain type and size.
Hard Copy	Paper copy.
Hardware	The equipment.
Input	Information that is entered into a system; to enter information into a system.
Interface	The connection of two or more systems or devices.
I/O	Input/Output.
Keyboarding	Typewriting.
Menu	A selection of tasks.
Modem	Hardware that connects the computer to telephone lines for sending and receiving information.
Output	The final results that are produced.
Software	Programs and routines needed to give instructions to the hardware.
Station	The work location of an operator.
Store	Place in memory or on disk.
Terminal	A device that can send and receive information.
Turnaround Time	The time that elapses from the beginning to the completion of a task.
Variable	A segment of text that is subject to change.
VDT	Video display terminal (same as CRT).

GENERAL SPELLING RULES

The following rules, without all the exceptions, provide a general guide to correct spelling and are adequate in most cases. When in doubt, use a good dictionary.

1. **Adding Prefixes and Suffixes**
   A. A prefix is one or more letters added to the beginning of a word to change its meaning:

   il + legal = illegal   un + noticed = unnoticed
   im + mortal = immortal   dis + approve = disapprove

   B. A suffix is one or more letters added to the end of a word to change its meaning:

   sing + er = singer   pay + able = payable
   usual + ly = usually   heat + ing = heating

   C. Words may be divided at the end of a line on the prefix: de-duct, pre-paid, re-lease; or on the root: fly-ing, near-est, room-mate. A root is a word from which others are derived. Fly is the root of flying; near is the root of nearest; room is the root of roommate.

2. **Doubling Final Consonants**
   A. In words of one syllable ending in a vowel and a consonant (except *h* or *x*), double the final consonant before *ed, er, est, ing:*

   plan   planned   planner   planning
   hot   hotter   hottest

   B. In words of more than one syllable ending in a vowel and a consonant and accented on the last syllable, follow the same rule as for words of one syllable: Double the final consonant before *ed, er, est, ing:*

   control   controlled   controller   controlling   controllable
   regret   regretted   regretting   regrettable

3. **EI or IE?**
   A. Write *ei* after *c* when the sound is *ee:* deceit, deceive, ceiling, conceive, perceive, receive, receipt

   B. Write *ie* after other letters: belief, believe, chief, fiend, grief, mischief, pierce, relieve, reprieve, shriek, sieve
   EXCEPTIONS: counterfeit, feign, foreign, forfeit, freight, height, heinous, leisure, neighbor, neither, reign, seize, sleigh, their, veil, vein, weight, weird

4. **Final E**
   A. Write the final *e* before a suffix beginning with a consonant:
   hope-hopeful; care-careless; manage-management
   EXCEPTIONS: awe-awful; due-duly; whole-wholly; judge-judgment; argue-argument; acknowledge-acknowledgment

Personal Computer (PC)

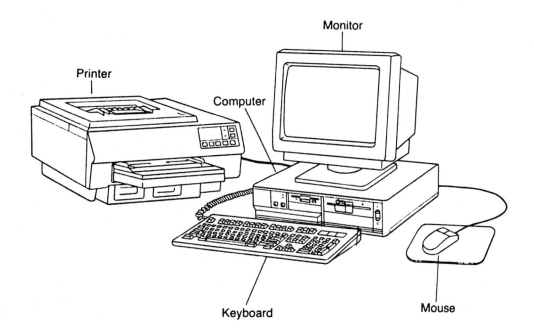

Courtesy of IBM.

Keyboard	The placement of alphabetic and numeric keys are standard and conform to any typewriter keyboard. Many keyboards have an additional ten-key numeric pad (similar to a calculator) for faster numeric entry.
Computer	The "brains" of the unit that receives commands from the keyboard. It serves as the central location for the storage and processing of data.
Monitor	The monitor, also known as a CRT, display screen, or VDT, is a television-like screen for the display of text.
Mouse	A small plastic box with buttons that connects to the computer. It can be used to replace the keyboard for many functions.
Printer	The printer, which gives you paper copy.

RULES FOR TYPING NUMBERS

Type in Figures:

1. All sums of money—round numbers without ciphers:

   Max borrowed $2,175 to buy a car.
   Her ballpoint pen costs 98 cents.

2. Percentages and decimals:

   The highest rate was 4.8 percent.

3. Numbers after nouns:

   Act 4; Scene 2; Track 6; Room 12.

4. House numbers, except house number One:

   Paul moved to 325 Stanton Street.
   Walt moved to One Delaney Street.

5. Measures, weights, distances, degrees, dimensions:

   10 quarts; 125 pounds; 650 miles.
   The temperature is 8° Fahrenheit.
   Our living room is 14 by 25 feet.

6. Numbers above ten:

   We ordered 11 more Spanish books.

7. Order, Invoice, Policy, Serial numbers—all without commas:

   Order No. 1623; Invoice No. 4958;
   Policy No. 5670; Serial No. 2079.

8. Numbers above ten used as street names. Endings **th, nd, st,** should be omitted:

   Ben lives at 50 West 11 Street.
   Ralph lives at 39-68 52 Avenue.
   Josephine lives at 472 91 Road.

9. Numbers and fractions in a series:

   Ship 5 bags, 10 boxes, 15 crates.
   1/2, 2/3, 3/4, 1/9, 2 5/6, 10 3/5

10. Time used with a.m. and p.m.*:

    We plan to arrive home at 10 p.m.

11. The larger of two numbers used together:

    Robert needs 50 five-cent stamps.

12. Exact age in years, months, days:

    15 years 10 months 17 days old.

13. Graduation and historical dates:

    The class of '57. Spirit of '76.

14. Decades and centuries:

    The gay 1890's. The 9th century.

*May also be used as AM and PM without periods.

Type in Words:

1. A number that begins a sentence:

   Seventy boys entered the contest.

2. Round numbers, except when used in advertising:

   About one hundred men were there.
   Our sale offers you 100 bargains.

3. Approximate ages:

   Dr. Hartley is about thirty-five.

4. Isolated numbers ten and lower:

   Sidney lived ten years in Berlin.

5. Numbers ten and lower used as street names:

   Martin lives at 490 Tenth Avenue.

6. Numbers used as proper names:

   David is in the Twelfth Regiment.

7. Indefinite sums of money:

   Al needs several hundred dollars.

8. Fractions standing alone:

   Mark ran three-fourths of a mile.

9. Numbers 10 and lower, *except* when used with numbers above 10:

   We need 25 books on English; 9 on Mathematics; 7 on Economics; 8 on French; 4 on Drawing; 3 on Latin. I will need at least four copies.

10. Time of day used informally:
    Time of day used with o'clock:

    I saw Jim at a quarter past four.
    Meet me at seven o'clock tonight.

STEP 1: HOW TO USE YOUR TYPEWRITER

1. Slide the paper guide to "0" on the paper-guide scale.

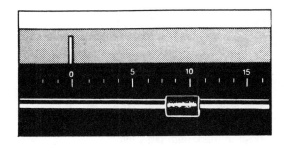

2. Set the line-space regulator for the required spacing.

   Single is 1 or –
   Double is 2 or =

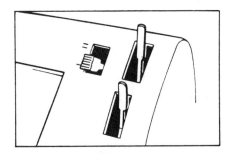

3. Pull the paper bail away from the cylinder.

RULES FOR PUNCTUATION SPACING

Space Once

1. After a comma: `Mary is tall, blond, and pretty.`
2. After a semicolon: `You must study; or you may fail.`
3. After an abbreviation: `Prof. Smythe will lecture today.`
4. Before and after the symbol **&:**   `We bought it at Grove & Roberts.`
5. After an exclamation mark within a sentence: `Whew! how those jets zip across.`
6. After a question mark within a sentence: `Where are my books? my supplies?`
7. Between a whole number and a "made" fraction: `The red rug is 12 3/4 feet long.`
   `(BUT:  The rug is 12½ feet long.)`
8a. After a sentence if you are using a computer   `I can do it. Can you? Show me.`

> NOTE: Do not space after the whole number if the fraction is on the keyboard.

Space Twice

8b. After a sentence if you are using a typewriter   `I can do it.  Can you?  Show me.`
9. After a colon, *except* when indicating time: ` Our need:  five new typewriters.`
   `Michael works from 8:30 to 4:30.`

Do Not Space

10. Before or after an apostrophe: `I borrowed my friend's overcoat.`
11. Before or after a decimal point: `Joe's savings amount to $629.50.`
12. Between parentheses and the words they enclose: `David Bowers (my pal) amuses me.`
13. Between quotation marks and the words they enclose: ` Jack said, "I'll see you later."`
14. Before or after a hyphen: `My daughter-in-law is a teacher.`
15. Before or after a dash: `Vic wrote Fay--at my suggestion.`
16. Before or after a comma in long numbers: `We sold 2,980,745 yards of silk.`
17. Before the symbol %:   `Our 5% bonds fall due next week.`
18. Between the symbol # and numerals: `Order #93 was shipped yesterday.`
    `The package weighed exactly 26#.`
19. After the period between small initials: `The show starts at 8 p.m. sharp.`
20. Before the symbols used for feet, inches, minutes, seconds: ` Mr. James Quincy is 5' 10" tall.`
    `Cal can run 850 yards in 1' 58".`

4. Insert standard 8-$\frac{1}{2}$" by 11" paper.

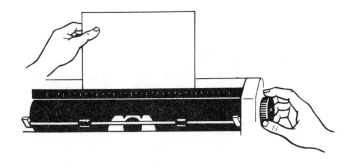

5a. See whether the paper is inserted straight.

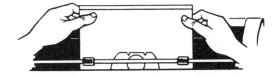

5b. If it is not, use the paper-release lever to straighten it.

8. **Geographical Names and Names of Buildings**
Capitalize geographical names and names of buildings:
```
East River
Atlantic Ocean
Rocky Mountains
Empire State Building
```

Do not capitalize east, west, north, or south when used to indicate direction:
```
Drive north on Broadway, then turn west on
42 Street.
```

9. **Companies, Organizations, Institutions, Government Agencies**
Capitalize the names of companies, organizations, institutions, and Government agencies:
```
Arco Publishing
American Automobile Association
Columbia University
Federal Communications Commission
```

10. **Nouns**
A. Capitalize a noun when it is part of a specific name:
```
Bentley School
```

B. Capitalize all proper nouns and their derivatives:
```
Mexico ................... Mexican
South ................... Southerner
Elizabeth ............... Elizabethan
```

11. **Languages, Religions, The Deity**
Capitalize languages, religions, and words denoting the Deity:
```
Spanish
Mohammedan
God
```

12. **Business Letters**
A. Address: Capitalize all titles in the address.
```
Mr. Harry Nevins, Manager
```

B. Salutation: Capitalize the first and last words, titles, and proper names in the salutation.
```
Dear Sir
Gentlemen
Dear Mr. Davis
```

C. Complimentary Close: Capitalize only the first word in the complimentary close.
```
Sincerely yours,
Yours very truly,
```

D. Closing Lines: Capitalize the title if it follows the name of the writer.
```
Thomas Ashton      Thomas Ashton, President
President
```

6. Leave a top margin of 1-$\frac{1}{2}$ inches—10 lines from the top of the page.

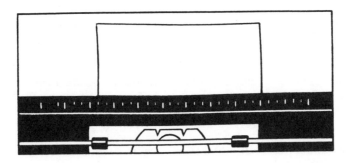

7. Set paper bail back in position.

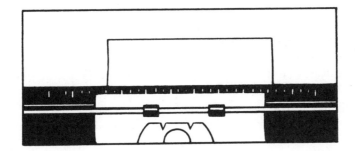

RULES FOR CAPITALIZATION

1. **General Rule**
   A. Capitalize the first word of a complete sentence:
      Mr. Hale is our office manager.

   B. Capitalize the first word of a quoted sentence:
      He said, "Mr. Hale is our office manager."

      NOTE: Do not capitalize the first word of a quotation if it is not a complete sentence:
      He said that Mr. Hale is "our office manager."

      Do not capitalize the first word of a quotation that is resumed within a sentence:
      "I'll phone Joe," she said, "while you dress."

2. **After a Colon**
   Capitalize the first word after a colon if that word begins a complete sentence:
   Here is Mr. Hale's message: Mail all the
   letters today.

3. **Titles of Persons**
   A. Capitalize a title when it applies to a specific person:
      President Nixon signed the welfare bill.

   B. Capitalize a title standing alone if it is of high distinction:
      The President vetoed the welfare bill.
      The Governor will speak to us tonight.

4. **Titles of Publications**
   (Books, Magazines, Newspapers, Articles, Plays, etc.)
   Capitalize the first word and every important word in the title:
   Sixty Years on the Firing Line (book)
   Death of a Salesman (play)

5. **Dates, Months, Holidays**
   Capitalize the days of the week, months of the year, and holidays:
   Friday
   December
   Christmas

6. **Historical Documents, Events, Monuments**
   Capitalize historical documents, events, and monuments:
   Declaration of Independence
   Battle of Gettysburg
   Statue of Liberty

7. **Seasons of the Year**
   Do not capitalize: spring . . . summer . . . autumn . . . winter

8. To remove the paper, move the paper-release lever toward you. Gently pull out the paper. Then move the lever back in place.

9. If you are using a typewriter with a moving carriage, you must center the carriage. Hold the cylinder knob, press the carriage-release lever, move the carriage to the center of the carriage scale, and remove your hand from the lever.

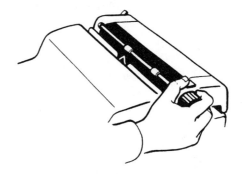

NOTE: If you are using an electric typewriter, remember to turn it off.

6. Use a hyphen with **ex** and **elect**:
   ```
   ex-President Johnson
   Mayor-elect Lindsay
   ```

7. Use a hyphen to avoid a confusing union of letters:
   ```
   re-enter
   pro-ally
   ```

8. Use a hyphen in compound nouns consisting of three or more words:
   ```
   brother-in-law
   teacher-in-charge
   ```

9. Use a hyphen in compound words beginning with **self**:
   ```
   a self-explanatory letter
   a self-addressed envelope
   ```

10. Use a hyphen in a series of hyphenated words having the same ending:
    ```
    We get first-, second-, and third-class mail.
    ```

The Dash

1. Use a dash to indicate an abrupt break in a sentence:
   ```
   Mr. Pearson left--where did he go?
   ```

2. Use a dash for emphasis:
   ```
   Type two hyphens--without spacing--for a dash.
   ```

3. Use a dash to set off a short, final summary:
   ```
   She had only one pleasure--dancing.
   ```

4. Use a dash to indicate the name of an author after a direct quotation:
   ```
   "To sin by silence when they should protest
   makes cowards out of men."--Abraham Lincoln
   ```

5. Use a dash to set off an explanatory group of words:
   ```
   His food--nuts, berries, fish--kept him alive.
   ```

NOTE: If you are using a computer, there is a symbol called an em dash, which takes the place of two hyphens.

STEP 2: GET READY TO TYPE

1. Clear your workstation of everything you do not need.

2. Prop your typing book in an upright position.

3. Sit all the way back on your chair. Your back should be straight.

4. Place your feet flat on the floor.

5. Place your elbows close to your body. Your forearms should be parallel to the keyboard.

6. Your wrists should be low, just clearing the keyboard.

7. Your body should be centered opposite the J-key.

8. Hold your head erect, facing your book.

9. *Left Hand*
   Place your fingertips on the **A S D F** keys. Draw the left thumb close to the first finger.

10. *Right Hand*
    Place your fingertips on the **J K L ;** keys. Extend your right thumb above the center of the space bar.

    Hint: In order to avoid stress to your body, it is important to move around every 15–20 minutes.

Courtesy of Grahl Industries, Clearwater, MI.

Parentheses

1. Use parentheses to enclose explanatory or added information:
   ```
   In our office (and in most offices) the
   full block style business letter is used.
   ```

2. Use parentheses to enclose enumerated items:
   ```
   Employers seek workers who are (1) accurate,
   (2) dependable, and (3) productive.
   ```

3. Use parentheses to enclose figures after amounts that are spelled out:
   ```
   The monthly rent is two hundred dollars ($200).
   ```

Question Mark

1. Use a question mark after a direct question:
   ```
   Do you know his address?
   ```

   But: After a question which is in the form of a request, use a period.
   ```
   May we have your check next week.
   Will you please mail an estimate.
   ```

2. Use a question mark with parentheses to express doubt or uncertainty concerning a statement immediately preceding:
   ```
   He was born May 10, 1892 (?).
   ```

Exclamation Point

1. Use an exclamation point to express strong feeling or emotion:
   ```
   Welcome home, son!
   Rush, it's urgent!
   ```

The Hyphen

1. Use a hyphen to divide a word at the end of a line. Make the division between syllables. Never type a hyphen at the beginning of a line.

2. Use a hyphen to join words serving as a single adjective *before* a noun:
   ```
   He is a well-known writer.
   ```

3. Use a hyphen in spelling fractions serving as modifiers:
   ```
   The job is two-thirds done.
   ```

   But: Two thirds of the job is done.

4. Use a hyphen in spelling the compound numbers twenty-one through ninety-nine.

5. Use a hyphen to form compound verbs:
   ```
   Double-check every entry.
   Do not side-step your duty.
   ```

LESSON 1
HOME KEYS

A S D F   J K L ;
Left hand   Right hand

COMPUTER MARGINS: 1" (left and right)
TYPEWRITER MARGINS: 15–70 (Pica)
25–80 (Elite)
SPACING: Single

Compare this type with the print on your machine.

```
This is Pica type:  10 characters per inch (cpi)*
This is Elite type:  12 characters per inch
```
This is proportional spacing: If you are using a computer, you can use spacing similar to that on a typeset page.

*A character is any letter, number, punctuation mark, or space on a line.

HOW TO STRIKE THE KEYS

Tap each key lightly and quickly using a flat-oval motion. Hold your fingers slightly above (not on) the keys. The keys respond instantly to very light strokes.

Follow each numbered step exactly.

1. **F-Key Tryout:** *Use Left First Finger.*
   Type the following **f**'s:

   ```
   ffffffffff
   ```

2. **J-Key Tryout:** *Use Right First Finger.*
   Type the following **j**'s:

   ```
   jjjjjjjjjj
   ```

3. **Space Bar Tryout:** *Use Side of Right Thumb.*
   To leave a space after a letter or a word, strike the space bar sharply with the side of your right thumb.

   Type the following **f j** alternately. Space sharply after each letter. Bounce the thumb off the space bar.

   ```
   ffffffffffjjjjjjjjjj f j f j f j f j f j f j f j
   ```

The Apostrophe

1. Use an apostrophe to show possession:
   (a) In singular and plural nouns not ending in *s*, add *'s*:
   ```
   boy's shoes
   men's coats
   ```

   (b) In singular nouns ending in *s*, add an apostrophe only:
   ```
   Dickens' novels
   Charles' papers
   OR add 's:  Dickens's novels
               Charles's papers
   ```
   The first form seems preferred. Both are correct.

   (c) In plural nouns ending in *s*, add an apostrophe only:
   ```
   lawyers' offices
   ```

   NOTE: In plural company and organization names that are possessive, omit the apostrophe:
   ```
   Teachers College
   Bankers Trust Co.
   ```

   (d) In compound words, add *'s*:
   ```
   father-in-law's car
   ```

   (e) In joint ownership, add *'s* to the last name only:
   ```
   Sue and Laura's room
   ```

   (f) In separate ownership, add *'s* to each name:
   ```
   Sue's and Laura's rooms
   ```

   (g) In indefinite pronouns, add *'s*:
   ```
   one's best efforts
   each other's rights
   ```

   NOTE: Do not use an apostrophe with possessive personal pronouns:
   ```
   his, hers, its, ours, yours, theirs
   ```

2. Use an apostrophe to indicate a contraction:
   ```
   isn't (is not)
   wasn't (was not)
   ```

3. Use an apostrophe to indicate feet and minutes after figures:
   ```
   Hy made the mile in 5'.
   The block is 125' long.
   ```

4. Use an apostrophe to indicate the omission of numbers:
   ```
   the spirit of '76
   ```

5. Use an apostrophe to indicate plurals of figures and letters:
   ```
   5's
   A's
   ```

4. **Return Practice:**

Note: On a computer keyboard, the [return] key will be an [Enter] key.

A. Swiftly extend the little finger of your right hand to the return key.
B. Lightly tap the return key, making the return automatically to the margin.
C. Move the finger back home.

Type the following line 5 times.

`fff jjj fff jjj fff jjj fff jjj fff jjj fff jjj fj`

Try to do the A B C steps (above) in one quick 1-2-3 motion.

5. **Home-Key Practice:** Type the following lines exactly. Double space after each 2-line group by using the return key twice. Doing so will leave one blank line between groups. The margin bell tells you that you are getting close to the right margin stop.

FIRST FINGER:	`fff jjj fff jjj fff jjj fff jjj fff jjj fff jjj fj` `fff jjj fff jjj fff jjj fff jjj fff jjj fff jjj fj`	Return to the margin without
SECOND FINGER:	`ddd kkk ddd kkk ddd kkk ddd kkk ddd kkk ddd kkk dk` `ddd kkk ddd kkk ddd kkk ddd kkk ddd kkk ddd kkk dk`	spacing at end of a line.
THIRD FINGER:	`sss lll sss lll sss lll sss lll sss lll sss lll sl` `sss lll sss lll sss lll sss lll sss lll sss lll sl`	
FOURTH FINGER:	`aaa ;;; aaa ;;; aaa ;;; aaa ;;; aaa ;;; aaa ;;; a;` `aaa ;;; aaa ;;; aaa ;;; aaa ;;; aaa ;;; aaa ;;; a;`	

NOTE: When you are using a computer you will have a wordwrap feature. This means that if text is too long to fit on a line, the next complete word will automatically return (wrap) to the left margin of the next line.

4. Use a colon after such expressions as **namely, for example, as follows,** if a series or a statement follows:

```
We shall place our order with you on one condition,
namely:  The entire lot must be shipped within ten
days after receipt of the order.
```

5. Use a colon after the salutation in business letters for mixed punctuation:

```
Dear Sir:
Dear Mr. Smith:
Gentlemen:
```

Quotation Marks

1. Use quotation marks to enclose titles of articles, plays, poems, essays, lectures, and the like:

```
I have read the article "Campus Revolution."
```

2. Use quotation marks to enclose direct quotations:

```
Emerson said, "The only way to have a
friend is to be one."
```

3. Use quotation marks to enclose each separate speech:

```
"I am sure," he said, "that we have met before."
```

   Rule: Put the comma and period inside quotation marks.

4. Use quotation marks to enclose special words—for emphasis:

```
I will check "debit"; you will check "credit."
Our company's "slogan":  QUALITY FIRST--ALWAYS
```

   Rule: Put the semicolon and colon outside quotation marks.

5. Use an apostrophe to enclose a quotation within a quotation:

```
Thomas said, "The command 'Don't give up
the ship' was given by John Paul Jones."
```

6. In a long quotation, use quotation marks only at the beginning of each paragraph and at the end of the last paragraph.

7. WITH QUESTION MARK
   A. If the entire sentence is a question, put the question mark outside the quotation marks:

```
Did Harry say, "I have just mailed the letter"?
```

   B. If only the quotation is a question, put the question mark inside the quotation marks:

```
Mr. Farley inquired, "Has the manager arrived?"
```

8. WITH EXCLAMATION MARK
   A. If the entire sentence is an exclamation, put the exclamation mark outside the quotation marks:

```
How foolish it is for the neighbors to "argue"!
```

   B. If only the quotation is an exclamation, put the exclamation mark inside the quotation marks:

```
Ken Riley shouted, "Dave hit another home run!"
```

6. **Test Your Skill:** Type the following lines exactly. Double space after each 2-line group by using the return key twice.

```
fff aaa ddd fad fad fad; jjj aaa lll jal jal jal;    Space once
fff aaa ddd fad fad fad; jjj aaa lll jal jal jal;    after a
                                                     semicolon.

aaa lll aaa lll all all; ddd aaa ddd dad dad dad;
aaa lll aaa lll all all; ddd aaa ddd dad dad dad;

sss aaa ddd sad sad sad; aaa sss kkk ask ask ask;
sss aaa ddd sad sad sad; aaa sss kkk ask ask ask;


a fad; ask dad; ask a lad; jal asks; a lad falls;    All the
a fad; ask dad; ask a lad; jal asks; a lad falls;    home keys.

all fads; alda asks; a sad lass; jal asks a lass;
all fads; alda asks; a sad lass; jal asks a lass;
```

8. Use a comma to separate thousands, millions, billions—except in order numbers, invoice numbers, serial numbers, policy numbers:

   3,791   25,132   4,392,690   2,365,930,038

9. Use a comma between title and name of organization if **of** or **of the** has been omitted:

   ```
   President, New York University
   Superintendent, Board of Education
   ```

10. Use a comma before conjunctions such as **and, but, for, or, neither,** and **nor** when they join two independent clauses:

    ```
    Many are called, but few are chosen.
    Ted shaved quickly, for he was late.
    ```

The Semicolon

1. Use a semicolon between independent clauses not joined by a conjunction:

   ```
   We may not go after all; we may stay home.
   ```

2. Use a semicolon between clauses joined by parenthetical expressions such as **therefore, however, otherwise, nevertheless** if the expression could start a new sentence:

   ```
   Mr. Roe is very well-known here; nevertheless, we cannot extend
   unlimited credit to him.
   ```

   NOTE: Use a comma after the parenthetical expression.

3. Use a semicolon to separate a series of phrases or clauses that contain one or more commas:

   ```
   The boys enjoyed their vacation in many ways; in the
   morning, by fishing; in the afternoon, by playing
   tennis; and in the evening, by indoor games.
   ```

4. Use a semicolon before such introductory expressions as **for example, namely, such as:**

   ```
   You need to do much research before you can write
   the speech; for example, you must read some books
   on the subject.
   ```

5. Use a semicolon to connect two short related sentences:

   ```
   Let's camp here; there's a lake nearby.
   ```

The Colon

1. Use a colon to introduce a listing when "the following" is mentioned or implied—except following the verb:

   ```
   I bought these items:  a tie, a shirt, and a hat.
   My favorite subjects are typing, gym, and English.
   ```

2. Use a colon to introduce a question:

   ```
   What I wish to know is:  Are you a touch typist?
   ```

   NOTE: Capitalize the first word after the colon if it is part of a complete sentence.

3. Use a colon to separate hours and minutes in expressing time:

   ```
   We arrived home at 2:30 a.m.
   ```

LESSON 2
NEW KEYS
E U

1. **Review:** Type each line twice. Double space after each 2-line group.

```
fff jjj ddd kkk sss lll aaa ;;; fdsa jkl; fdsajkl;
fad fad jal jal sad sad lad lad dad dad asks asks;
add add; dad dad; fall fall; asks asks; lass lass;
ask ada; ask jal; dad asks a lad; a sad lad falls;
ask a lad; jal asks a sad lad; a sad lad asks dad;
```

Always keep eyes on copy. Think the finger and the key it controls.

2. **New-Key Practice: E** *Use D-Finger.*
Practice the reach from **D** to **E** and back home to **D**. Keep the **A**-finger on its home key. When you can reach **E** without looking at your fingers, type each line twice:

Double space after each 2-line group.

```
e e e e ded ded ded ded; fed fed fed; led led led;
ded ded ded elk elk elk; jed jed jed; elf elf elf;
ded ded ded fee fee fee; see see see; ale ale ale;
ded ded ded lea lea lea; sea sea sea; eke eke eke;
fed led elk jed elf fee; see ale lea; sea jed eel;
```

Space once after a semicolon.

3. **New-Key Practice: U** *Use J-Finger.*
Practice the reach from **J** to **U** and back home to **J**. Keep the **L** and **;** fingers on their home keys. When you can reach **U** without looking at your fingers, type each line twice:

```
u u u u juj juj juj juj; dud dud dud; due due due;
juj juj juj uke uke uke; use use use; sue sue sue;
juj juj juj jud jud jud; ula ula ula; auk auk auk;
juj juj juj flu flu flu; due due due; sud sud sud;
use dud due sud jud flu; eke auk ula; sue due use;
```

Return fingers quickly to home keys.

Lesson 2: E U

9

RULES FOR PUNCTUATION

The Period

1. Use a period after a statement:
   The material will be shipped today.

2. Use a period after an abbreviation:
   Mr. Bradley is moving to St. Louis.

3. Use a period for a decimal point in numbers:
   Our overtime rate is $4.50 an hour.

4. Use a period after each initial in a person's name, spacing only once:
   Mr. E. S. Goldman will call on you.

The Comma

1. Use a comma to separate words, phrases, or clauses in a series:
   The display consists of rings, watches, and bracelets.
   Mary will shop for you, cook for you, and sew for you.

2. Use a comma after an introductory word, phrase, or clause:
   However, I am inclined to agree with you.
   In the meantime, we have decided to wait.
   After I endorsed the check, he mailed it.

3. Use a comma to set off a word, phrase, or clause that is not essential to the thought in a sentence:
   Our manager, Mr. Ralph Dix, is on vacation.
   Her mother, who is in Paris, telephoned me.

4. Use a comma to set off words in direct address:
   Will you, Mr. Hampton, write the letter?

5. Use a comma before short direct quotations:
   He said, "I am leaving for London tomorrow."

6. Use a comma to indicate the omission of a word:
   Henry is tall; Walter, short.

7. Use a comma to separate two words or figures that may be confusing:
   To Robert, Thomas was a perfect gentleman.
   In 1941, 30 ships were lost in one day.
   Instead of 25, 52 men applied for the job.

4. **Boost Your Skill:**
   A. Type each line 3 times.
   B. Practice words that have errors.
   C. Try for a PERFECT copy of both lines.

   All the keys you know.

   ```
   ask sue; a full fee; use a desk; see a jade flask;
   feed jal a salad; sue sells flasks; ella asks sue;
   ```

   Type at a steady, even pace.

REFERENCE GUIDE

RULES FOR WORD DIVISION

1. Divide a word only between syllables, provided you are not breaking a root word — con-sist / pass-ing

2. Divide a word between double consonants — mat-ter

   NOTE: If a word is derived from a word already ending in a double consonant, divide it after the second consonant — add-ing

3. Divide a word after a prefix of more than one letter — pre-scribe

4. Divide a word before a suffix of more than one letter — lead-ing

5. Divide a word between two vowels coming together — gradu-ation

6. Divide a word after a vowel—if the vowel is a separate syllable — regu-lar

7. Divide a word between two consonants coming between two vowels — impor-tant

8. Divide a hyphenated word only on the hyphen — self-esteem

   NOTE: All words beginning with **self** are hyphenated, except **selfish.**

9. Do not divide a one-syllable word — passed

10. Do not divide a word with fewer than 6 letters.

11. Do not divide these endings: **able   cient   cial   sion   eous**
    tion   ible   cious   tial

12. Do not divide a capitalized word — Chicago

13. Do not divide a word unless you can carry 2 or 3 letters to the next line — bet-ter

14. Do not separate: (a) mixed numbers — 150 3/4
    (b) sums of money — $125.50

15. Do not separate one letter from the rest of a word. You cannot divide **about, around.**

16. Do not divide: (a) contractions — hasn't
    (b) abbreviations — C.O.D.

17. Avoid dividing the last word of a paragraph or page.

18. Avoid dividing the last word on the first line of a paragraph or page.

19. Avoid separating: (a) parts of a name — Sam Jones
    (b) title from name — Dr. Jones

20. Avoid dividing any word—if possible.

    When in doubt, find out: Consult the dictionary.

LESSON 3
NEW KEYS
R I

COMPUTER MARGINS: 1" (left and right)
TYPEWRITER MARGINS: 15–70 (Pica)
25–80 (Elite)
SPACING: Single

1. **Review:** Type each line twice. Double space after each 2-line group.

```
fff jjj ddd kkk sss lll aaa ;;; ded juj ded juj eu
ale elk jud use jake dues fuel fuse fake sulk jade
ask sue; a full fee; use a desk; see a jade flask;
a lad sees; a lad sees a duel; jud sells us seeds;
see us; sue sees us; use a desk; use a full flask;
```

Space quickly.

Keep elbows close to body.

2. **New-Key Practice: R** *Use F-Finger.*
    Practice the reach from **F** to **R** and back home to **F**. Keep the **A S D** fingers in home position.
    When you can reach **R** without looking at your fingers, type each line twice.

Remember: Double space after each 2-line group.

```
r r r r frf frf frf frf; fur fur fur; jar jar jar;
frf frf frf are are are; ark ark ark; red red red;
frf frf frf rue rue rue; ear ear ear; ref ref ref;
frf frf frf era era era; ere ere ere; far far far;
red ark fur rue jar ref ear raj era are ruse lurk;
```

Type the first copy of each line slowly; then a little faster on the second.

Return to the margin without looking up.

3. **New-Key Practice: I** *Use K-Finger.*
    Practice the reach from **K** to **I** and back home to **K**. Keep semicolon-finger in home position.
    When you can reach **I** without looking at your fingers, type each line twice.

```
i i i i kik kik kik kik; irk irk irk; sir sir sir;
kik kik kik kid kid kid; air air air; fir fir fir;
kik kik kik rid rid rid; ail ail ail; lid lid lid;
kik kik kik die die die; aid aid aid; lie lie lie;
air fir kid sir rid rue lid lie aid ail sail jail;
```

12 Tips for Careful Proofreading

Your ability to proofread is critical. One typographical error (known as a *typo*) or one improperly placed punctuation mark can completely change the meaning of your message.

> *Typo (*w* instead of *t*)*
>
> I will now go to the meeting.
>
> I will not go to the meeting.
>
> *Improperly placed colon*
>
> Execution: impossible to be pardoned
>
> Execution impossible: to be pardoned

The following are hints for proofreading thoroughly and accurately.

1. Scan the document with an eye for format and style.
    Example: If you used the full block letter style, is everything left justified?

2. Check the spelling of people's names, including middle initials and titles.
    Example: Did you write *Mr.* instead of *Ms.* or spell *Glenn* with two n's instead of one?

3. Pay special attention to numbers.
    Example: Did you tell the reader he/she owes you $7,115.00 instead of $7,515.00?

4. Keep an eye out for misused or misspelled homonyms.
    Example: Did you use *their* instead of *there*?

5. Look for repeated words.
    Example: Perhaps you wrote, "I will call Mr. Jones in in a week."

6. Be on the alert for small words that are misspelled. We tend to read what we know should be there.
    Example: It's easy to type *at* instead of *as* and not notice the error.

7. Check dates.
    Example: If you wrote Monday, July 10, be certain July 10 is a Monday.

8. Check for omissions.
    Example: Did you leave off an area code, zip code, or other critical piece of information?

9. If you're proofreading a technical or statistical document, it's best to use the buddy system. If no one is available to help, read the document with a ruler (line by line) checking it against the source of the information.

10. If you're working on a computer, use the spell checker. It won't catch everything (such as misspelled names) but it will catch a lot.

11. If you're working on a typewriter, you might try reading from bottom to top or from right to left.

12. Re-read the document after you've gotten some distance from working on it.
    Example: Re-read it the following day if time allows. If not, take a five- or ten-minute break, then re-read it.

4. **Boost Your Skill:**
   A. Type each line 3 times.
   B. Practice words that have errors.
   C. Try for a PERFECT copy of both lines.

   ```
   all is fair; sell us jars; a kid used a real idea;  All the keys
   fill a jar; fill a red jar; fill all red jars full  you know.
   ```

M E M O R A N D <del>A</del> ~UM~

To: All Personn~ale~ *nel*

From: Marc A. Laurence

Date: September 30, 19--

   Subject: Office Supplies ⌐margin

It has come to my attention that many office supplies ~has~ have been missing lately. Now that many of your ~kids~ are ∧children back in school for the Fall term, the condition has worsened.

Unfortunately, you have left me no choice but to enforce the following policy: No∧one is allowed in the supply room without my secretary, Miss Sullivan, accompanying them. ~Me and~ She and I ~her~ are the only ones who will have keys to the supply room.

We deeply regret having to take this action, but we are certain that you will see why it is necessary.

   sll

M E M O R A N D U M

To: All Personnel

From: Marc A. Laurence

Date: September 30, 19--

Subject: Office Supplies

It has come to my attention that many office supplies have been missing lately. Now that many of your children are back in school for the fall term, the condition has worsened.

Unfortunately, you have left me no choice but to enforce the following policy: No one is allowed in the supply room without my secretary, Miss Sullivan, accompanying them. She and I are the only ones who will have keys to the supply room.

We deeply regret having to take this action, but we are certain that you will see why it is necessary.

   sll

LESSON 4
NEW KEYS
G O

COMPUTER MARGINS: 1" (left and right)
TYPEWRITER MARGINS: 15–70 (Pica)
                        25–80 (Elite)
SPACING: Single

1. **Review:** Type each line twice. Double space after each 2-line group.

    ```
    frf juj ded kik sss lll aaa ;;; frf juj ded kik ri    Hit space
    sir rue lid due ail jar kid ire fur auk jerk raid;    bar.
    all is fair; sell us jars; a kid used a real idea;
    russ is ill; fred uses skill; jed said alf is safe
    all kids; all kids like; all kids sure like sleds;
    ```

2. **New-Key Practice: G** *Use F-Finger.*
    Practice the reach from **F** to **G** and back home to **F**. Keep the **A S D** fingers in home position. When you can reach **G** without looking at your fingers, type each line twice:

    ```
    g g g g fgf fgf fgf fgf; jug jug jug; rug rug rug;    Move
    fgf fgf fgf dig dig dig; leg leg leg; fig fig fig;    fingers back
    fgf fgf fgf sag sag sag; dug dug dug; gag gag gag;    to home
    rig rig rig egg egg egg; jig jig jig; keg keg keg;    keys.
    jug jig rug fig age lug jag gas keg rag flag glad;
    ```

3. **New-Key Practice: O** *Use L-Finger.*
    Practice the reach from **L** to **O** and back home to **L**. Keep the **J**-finger in home position. When you can reach **O** without looking at your fingers, type each line twice:

    ```
    o o o o lol lol lol lol; old old old; oaf oaf oaf;
    lol lol lol dog dog dog; oak oak oak; oar oar oar;
    lol lol lol sol sol sol; jog jog jog; roe roe roe;
    log log log joe joe joe; oil oil oil; our our our;
    oil old dog jog sol log doe roe oaf foe golf goal;
    ```

The following memorandum contains many errors in both content and form. Use the proofreader's marks on page 131 to indicate the necessary changes. Then, type the memorandum correctly. (The corrections and the corrected memorandum appear on page 137.)

```
                        M E M O R A N D A


To:  All Personal

From:  Marc A. Laurence

Date:  September 30. 19--

     Subject:  Office Supplies


     It has come to my attension that many office supplies has
     have been missing latley.  Now that many of your kids are
     back in school for the Fall term, the condition has
     worstened.

     Unfortunately you have left me no choise but to enforse the
     following policy:  Noone is allowed in the supply room with
     out my secretary, Miss sullivan, accompanying them.  Me and
     her are the only one's who will have keys to the supply
     room.

     We deeply regret having to take this action but we are
     certain that you will see why it is necessary.

     sll
```

4. **Boost Your Skill:**
   A. Type each line 3 times.
   B. Practice words that have errors.
   C. Try for a PERFECT copy of both lines.

   gail uses jugs; gail uses old jugs for salad oils; All the keys
   joe seeks four dark jade rugs for four glad girls; you know.

12 Seventh Avenue
Ridgefield Park, NJ 07660
June 16, 19--

Mrs. Janice Teisch
Business Manager
Real World Counseling Service
134 Fourth Avenue
New York, NY 07081

Dear Mrs. Teisch:

Your sales manager, Bunny Feiler, has informed me that your
company will soon be adding to its secretarial staff. Please
consider me a candidate for one of the positions.

Your company could no doubt benefit from a person experienced in
dealing with the public and trained in shorthand and typing--in
addition to having a bookkeeping background.

Although my enclosed resume supports my claims, I know there will
be questions it cannot answer. May I request an interview at your
earliest convenience.

Sincerely yours,

Lynne Sullivan

Enclosure

Lesson 35: Proofreader's Marks

LESSON 5
NEW KEYS
Shift Keys . (Period)

COMPUTER MARGINS: 1" (left and right)
TYPEWRITER MARGINS: 15–70 (Pica)
                        25–80 (Elite)
SPACING: Single

1. **Review:** Type each line twice. Double space after each 2-line group.

All the keys
you know.

```
fdsa jkl; fdsa jkl; ask lad jal fad sad fall flask
frf juj ded kik fgf lol rig due old jugs kegs rode
all is fair; sell us jars; a kid used a real idea;
gail uses jugs; gail uses old jugs for salad oils;
joe seeks four dark jade rugs for four glad girls;
```

Keep your wrists as motionless as possible. Let your fingers do the work.

2. **New-Key Practice: Left Shift Key** *Use A-Finger.*
To capitalize a letter typed by your right hand:
(1) Stretch **A**-finger to shift key, keeping **F**-finger at home.
(2) Hold shift key down while you type letter to be capitalized.
(3) Release shift key—move fingers to home keys.

Type each line twice:

```
J J Ja Ja Jal Jal Jal; K K Ki Ki Kid Kid Kid;
L L Lo Lo Lou Lou Lou; U U Ul Ul Ula Ula Ula;
I I Id Id Ida Ida Ida; O O Ol Ol Ole Ole Ole;
```

Hold shift key down until you have struck and released the key for the capital letter.

```
                Seventh
        12 7th Avenue
        Ridgefield Park, NJ    07660 [2 Spaces
        June 16, 19--



        Mrs. Janice Teisch
        Business manager
        Real World Counseling Service
        134 Fourth Avenue
        New York, NY 07081
               Mrs.
        Dear Miss Teisch ⁄⊙

        Your sales manager, Bunny Feiler, has informed me that your your
        company will soon be adding to its secretarial staff. Please
        consider me a candidate for one of the positionS⊙
                                        e
        Your company no doubt could benifit from a person experienced in
        dealing with the public and trained in shorthand and typing--⌒in
        editions to having a bookkeeping background.
        addition                    ^
                                                    there
        Although my enclosed resume supports my claims, I know their will
        be questions it can⌒not answer.  May I request an interview at
        your earliest convenience.
                                    e
                        Sincerly yours,
                              ^          ⌈ at
                                         |
                                         | Margin
                        Lynne Sullivan   ⌊

   Enclosure
```

3. **New-Key Practice: Right Shift Key** *Use ;-Finger.*
   To capitalize a letter typed by your left hand:
   (1) Stretch **;**-finger to shift key, keeping **J**-finger at home.
   (2) Hold shift key down while you type letter to be capitalized.
   (3) Release shift key—move fingers to home keys.

Type each line twice:

F F Fa Fa Fae Fae Fae; G G Gu Gu Gus Gus Gus; Depress
D D De De Del Del Del; S S Sa Sa Sal Sal Sal; shift key
A A Al Al Alf Alf Alf; R R Ro Ro Rod Rod Rod; firmly.

4. **New-Key Practice: . (Period)** *Use L-Finger.*

Space once after the period.

Practice the reach from **L** to Period and back home to **L**. Curl the **L**-finger as it goes downward. Keep the **J**-finger in home position. When you can reach the period without looking at your fingers, type each line twice:

. . . . 1.1 1.1 1.1 1.1 Jr. Jr. Jr. Sr. Sr. Sr.
Dr. Dr. Dr. Ed. Ed. Ed. Fr. Fr. Fr. Rd. Rd. Rd.

Jr. for Junior
Sr. for Senior
Dr. for Doctor
Ed. for Editor
  or Education
Fr. for French
Rd. for Road

5. **Boost Your Skill:**
   A. Type each line twice—smoothly.
   B. Practice words that have errors.
   C. Start over. See how many perfect pairs of lines you can turn out.

All the keys you know.

Joel fed us. See Dr. Gold. Lou asked for a salad.
Gus seeks oil. Gus seeks a jug of oil for Gloria.
Lou sold all four dogs. Jo said dogs fear a gale.
Ed uses a desk file. A desk file is good for all.
All skills are good. All skills are good if used.

Space twice for a monospaced font or a typewriter. Space once for proportional spacing on a computer.

The following letter contains many errors in both content and form. Use the proofreader's marks on page 131 to indicate the necessary changes. Then, type the letter correctly. (The corrections appear on page 134, and the final letter is on page 135.)

12 7th Avenue
Ridgefield Park, NJ 07660
June 16, 19--

Mrs. Janice Teisch
Business manager
Real World Counseling Service
134 Fourth Avenue
New York, NY 07081

Dear Miss Teisch,

Your sales manager, Bunny Feiler, has informed me that your your company will soon be adding to its secretarial staff. Please consider me a candidate for one of the position.

Your company no doubt could benifit from a person expereinced in dealing with the public and trained in shorthand and typing-- in edition to having a bookeeping background.

Although my enclosed resume supports my claims, I know their will be questions it can not answer. May I request an interview at your earliest convenience.

Sincerly yours,

Lynne Sullivan

LESSON 6
NEW KEYS
T H

1. **Review:** Type each line twice. Double space after each 2-line group.

    fdsa jkl; fdsa jkl; ask sad lad jal fad fall flask   All the keys
    frf juj ded kik fgf lol rig due old jugs kegs rode   you know.
    Flo Gus Del Sue Alf Rod Ella Joe Kid Lou Ole Ulaf;
    Joe fed us. See Dr. Gold. Lou asked for a salad.   Return
    All skills are good. All skills are good if used.   to the
                                                         margin
                                                         without
                                                         looking up.

2. **New-Key Practice: T** *Use F-Finger.*
    Practice the reach from **F** to **T** and back home to **F**. Keep the **A** and **S** fingers in home
    position. When you can reach **T** without looking at your fingers, type each line twice:

    t t t t ftf ftf ftf ftf; fit fit fit; lot lot lot;   Eyes on
    ftf ftf ftf rut rut rut; jet jet jet; kit kit kit;   copy. Be a
    ftf ftf ftf tea tea tea; sit sit sit; tug tug tug;   touch
    toe toe toe dot dot dot; ate ate ate; jut jut jut;   typist.
    fit lot rut jet kit tea sit tug dot jut true tire;

3. **New-Key Practice: H** *Use J-Finger.*
    Practice the reach from **J** to **H** and back home to **J**. Keep the **K L ;** fingers in home position.
    When you can reach **H** without looking at your fingers, type each line twice:

    h h h h jhj jhj jhj jhj; hut hut hut; her her her;
    jhj jhj jhj hat hat hat; had had had; she she she;
    jhj jhj jhj hag hag hag; hoe hoe hoe; ash ash ash;
    hue hue hue hit hit hit; hot hot hot; the the the;
    hug hoe has hat hid she rush josh fish hook hills;

After the corrections have been made, the copy on page 131 will read as follows:

If you are planning to go to work in an office after graduation from high school, take all the business subjects offered. Typing, shorthand, English, business arithmetic, and bookkeeping are essential for most office jobs. They help a _beginner_ get a good start in the business world. Try to EXCEL in them.

Test your aptitude for office work while you are in school. Take part in its administrative, clerical, and bookkeeping functions. Also, try to get an office job during vacations. Whatever business experience you can get will give you a good chance to find out first hand what office work is like.

So prepare now by taking advantage of your high school years to build a firm foundation for SUCCESS.

4. **Boost Your Skill:**
   A. Type each line 3 times.
   B. Practice words that have errors.
   C. Try for a PERFECT copy of both lines.

   ```
   Joel got to that lake at four.  He hooked a trout.
   Ask Gil or Kurt to look for Hale at the old house.
   ```

5. **Figure Your Speed**   You can tell how fast you type by timing yourself, or by having someone time you.
   A. Note the word-count scale below. It shows that every 5 characters—letters, numbers, punctuation marks, and spaces—count as 1 average word. The scale shows that each of the 2 lines above it has 10 words.
   B. If you type the first line in 1 minute, your speed is 10 words a minute. If you type both lines in 1 minute, your speed is $2 \times 10 = 20$ words a minute.
   C. If you type part of a line, note the number below where you stopped; it tells you how many words to count for that part of the line.

   EXAMPLE: Let's say that in the 1-minute timing below, you typed the first line and had to stop after typing the word "right" in the second line. Your speed would be:

   10 words in line 1
   <u> 6</u> words in line 2
   16 words in 1 minute

6. **Test Your Skill:** Take Three 1-Minute Timings.

   Follow these steps in all your 1-minute timings.

   A. Repeat if you finish before end of 1 minute.
   B. After each timing, jot down total words typed and total errors. Count only 1 error in a word even if it has more.
   C. Practice the words that have errors till they are easy for you.
   D. Record on your Progress Chart for Timings (page 153) your best speed within 3 errors.
   Goal: 15 words a minute within 3 errors.

   WORDS

   All the keys you know.
   ```
   Jill has a silk skirt.  Her sister got it for her.    10
   The skirt fits her just right.  Dora likes it too.    20
        1    2    3    4    5    6    7    8    9    10
   ```

LESSON 35
PROOFREADER'S MARKS

You may sometimes have to type a revised copy of typed or printed matter. Some notations indicating the corrections will be self-explanatory; others will consist of special symbols known as proofreader's marks. These symbols are often used by writers, editors, and businesspeople. Each correction is indicated in the copy. Some of the more common symbols are illustrated below.

¶	Paragraph	#	Leave a space	∧	Insert
≋	Capital letter(s)	⌐	Move to left	⊙	Insert period
N or tr	Transpose	⌐	Move to right	⌃	Insert comma
℘	Take it out	lc	Small letter	⌃	Insert semicolon
stet	Don't change	⊔	Lower this letter	?	Insert question mark
⌣	Close up	⌐	Raise this letter	!	Insert exclamation mark

Placing Proofreader's Marks

¶ If you are planning to go ~~directly~~ to work in an office

after graduation from high school, take all the business

subjects offered. typing, shorthand, English, Business

arithmetic and bookkeeping are essential for most office

jobs. They help a beginner get a good start in the busi-

ness world. Try to ~~excel~~ in ~~these subjects~~.
                  excel   them

Test your aptitude for office work while you are in
                    stet
school. Take part in its ~~administrative~~, clerical, and

⌐bookkeeping functions. Also, try to get an office job

⌐during vacations. Whatever business experience you can get

will give you a good ch ance to find out first hand that
                                                      w
office work is like⊙
      #
Soprepare now by taking advantage of your high
    ∧
school years to build a firm foundation for success.

LESSON 7
NEW KEYS
W Y , (Comma)

COMPUTER MARGINS: 1" (left and right)
TYPEWRITER MARGINS: 15–70 (Pica)
                      25–80 (Elite)

SPACING: Single

1. **Review:** Type each line twice. Double space after each 2-line group.

```
fgf jhj fdsa jkl; fgf jhj fdsa jkl; fgf jhj fg jh;
frf juj ftf jhj fgf kik ded lol ss aa 1. 1. 1. 1.1
jug led for ask sag hit jet out sol tug goes salt;
Jill has a silk skirt.  Her sister got it for her.
The skirt fits her just right.  Dora likes it too.
```

Return fingers quickly to home keys. Keep elbows close to body.

2. **New-Key Practice: W** *Use S-Finger.*
   Practice the reach from **S** to **W** and back home to **S**. Keep the **F**-finger close to its home key. Try to hold elbow close to body. When you can reach **W** without looking at your fingers, type each line twice:

```
w w w w sws sws sws sws; sow sow sow; low low low;
sws sws sws was was was; few few few; row row row;
sws sws sws wag wag wag; how how how; jaw jaw jaw;
who who who wit wit wit; dew dew dew; awl awl awl;
dew row was law few wag how jaw wit wed work slow;
```

Type at a steady, even pace.

3. **New-Key Practice: Y** *Use J-Finger.*
   Practice the reach from **J** to **Y** and back home to **J**. Keep the **K L ;** fingers in home position. When you can reach **Y** without looking at your fingers, type each line twice:

```
y y y y jyj jyj jyj jyj; yet yet yet; yak yak yak;
jyj jyj jyj shy shy shy; sly sly sly; way way way;
jyj jyj jyj try try try; why why why; dry dry dry;
yes yes yes jay jay jay; sly sly sly; fry fry fry;
guy say dye you key lay joy toy hay day eye yield;
```

Use finger-reach action only; arms and hands quiet.

<u>WORKS CONSULTED</u>

Harwick, Arthur, <u>War and Social Change in the Twentieth Century</u>, New
York: St. Martin's Press, 1974.

Hawley, Ellis, <u>The Great War and the Search for a Modern Order</u>, New
York: St. Martin's Press, 1979.

Hicks, John, <u>Republican Ascendancy 1921–1933</u>, New York: Harper & Row,
1960.

Murphy, Paul L., <u>World War I and the Origin of Civil Liberties in the
United States</u>, New York: W. W. Norton & Company, 1923, 1979.

Snowman, Daniel, <u>America Since 1920</u>, New York: Harper & Row, 1968.

4. **New-Key Practice: , (Comma)** *Use K-Finger.*
   Practice the reach from **K** to **,** and back home to **K**. Curl the **K**-finger as it goes downward. Keep the **;**-finger in home position. When you can reach the **,** without looking at your fingers, type each line twice:

All the keys
you know.

```
, , , k,k k,k k,k yak, yak, yak; lark, lark, lark;   Space once
k,k k,k k,k work, work, work; sheik, sheik, sheik;   after a
jerk, fork, dark, silk, lurk, stork, freak, Greek;   comma and
                                                     semicolon.
```

5. **Boost Your Skill:**
   A. Type each line smoothly 3 times.
   B. Practice words that have errors.
   C. Try for a PERFECT copy of both lines.

```
Yes, Walt took the test.  He told Jud it was easy.   All the keys
Take the ferry, Edward.  You will get there early.   you know.
```

6. **Test Your Skill:** Take Three 1-Minute Timings.
   Goal: 15 words a minute within 3 errors.
   Record your best speed within 3 errors.

WORDS

All the keys
you know.
```
Try to do the work just right if you do it at all.    10
Good daily work is a sure way to get to your goal.    20
         1    2    3    4    5    6    7    8    9    10
```

Lesson 7: W Y , (Comma)   **20**

WORKS CITED

[1] Hawley, Ellis. *The Great War and the Search for a Modern Order*. (New York: St. Martin's Press, 1979), p. 3.

[2] Snowman, Daniel. *America Since 1920*. (New York: Harper & Row, 1968), p. 23.

[3] Hicks, John. *Republican Ascendancy 1921–1933*. (New York: Harper & Row, 1960), p. 85.

[4] Hawley, p. 26.

LESSON 8
NEW KEYS
Q P : (Colon)

COMPUTER MARGINS: 1" (left and right)
TYPEWRITER MARGINS: 15–70 (Pica)
                        25–80 (Elite)
SPACING: Single

1.   **Review:** Type each line twice. Double space after each 2-line group.

```
frf juj ftf jyj fgf jhj ded kik sws lol aaa ;;; wy    Type
kit yet lid why fir how use sir tow jig lye aid so    smoothly—
The daily drills will aid you to get to your goal.    without
Yes, Flora; Judith does her task with great skill.    pausing.
Walter told Jerry Hale that he hooked a huge fish.
```

2.   **New-Key Practice: Q** *Use A-Finger.*
     Practice the reach from **A** to **Q** and back home to **A**. Keep the **F**-finger on its home key. Keep elbow close to your side. When you can reach **Q** without looking at your fingers, type each line twice:

```
q q q q aqa aqa aqa aqa; aqua aqua; quotes quotes;    Sit straight.
aqa aqa aqa quit quit; quail quail; liquor liquor;    Keep wrists
aqa aqa aqa quay quay; quite quite; quaffs quaffs;    low without
aqa aqa aqa quid quid; quirk quirk; quires quires;    touching
quit quid quad quest quote quite quilt quash quake    machine.
```

3.   **New-Key Practice: P** *Use ;-Finger.*
     Practice the reach from **;** to **P** and back home to **;**. Keep the **J K** fingers close to their home keys. Keep elbow close to your side. When you can reach **P** without looking at your fingers, type each line twice:

```
p p p p ;p; ;p; ;p; ;p; pal pal pal; pit pit pits;    Keep right
;p; ;p; ;p; pay pay pay; par par par; pie pie pie;    thumb
;p; ;p; ;p; put put put; pig pig pig; paw paw paw;    curved,
pep pep pep sip sip sip; hip hip hip; fop fop fop;    close to the
lip fop sap hip gyp dip put kip paw rip jeep quip;    space bar.
```

One of the important results of the war was the gains made by the workers and trade unions. Before the war, unions had been looked upon as a source of local trouble that was to be dealt with by local authorities.

During the war, unions were successful in gaining higher wages through collective bargaining and arbitration--instead of through crippling strikes. This contributed to greater union membership and greater respect for unions. After the war there were occasions when strikes became necessary. The strike became a more powerful weapon because both industry and the public had become dependent upon unions. Thus, if a union threatened to strike, much greater consideration was paid to the union's demands than had been before the war.[3]

At the onset of the war, when industry was called upon to shift production into high gear, the response was confusion and disorder. The government was compelled to take temporary wartime control of some vital industries to insure maximum efficiency. While in control, the government instituted some good work policies that were carried over to peacetime and have survived right up to today. Some of these were as follows: an eight-hour work day, time and a half for overtime, less employee discontent, and expanded employee welfare benefits.[4]

4. **New-Key Practice: : (Colon)** *Use ;-Finger.*
   To type the colon, depress the left shift key and strike the ;-key.

Space twice after a colon, except when indicating time.

   EXAMPLES: Foods we like: grapes, eggs, soda.
              We also like: yogurt, fish, pears.

   Type each line twice:

   : : : ;:; ;:; ;:; Dear Gay: Dear Pal: Dear Kurt:
   Dear Joe: Walt stayed at Hotel Quill till Friday.

All the keys you know.

5. **Boost Your Skill:**
   A. Type each line 3 times—smoothly.
   B. Practice words that have errors.
   C. Try for a PERFECT copy of both lines.

Space once after period following a capital initial.

      Judge Paul K. Quale did free the slow, tired jury.
      Joe Yale will take Paula Quat to the party Friday.

6. **Test Your Skill:** Take Three 1-Minute Timings.
   Goal: 15 words a minute within 3 errors.
         Record your best speed within 3 errors.

   WORDS

All the keys
you know. Dear Joe: Gus Quill says he types all the letters   10
          for his father. This work surely tests his skill.   20
            1   2   3   4   5   6   7   8   9   10

METAMORPHOSIS--WORLD WAR I

If one studies history, one is at some point confronted with the question of what factors cause times of calm and those of rapid change. It is an irony of history that periods of great progress have often come immediately following war. Many wars have brought changes, but no war brought as much change as did World War I (WWI). WWI most changed the previously isolated United States. Through economic, social, and political change resulting from WWI, the United States developed into a world power.

INDUSTRIAL REVOLUTION

During the American Industrial Revolution, the economy grew tremendously. Industrial production per person rose three times, and national industrial production rocketed to eight times what it was in 1870.[1] England still remained the world's leading economic power, despite America's fantastic gains. When WWI broke out, the allies soon became dependent on American goods. American industries were called upon to be the "arsenal of democracy." Because of this demand,

> America emerged from the war as the world's leading economic power.[2]

LESSON 9
THE TABULATOR

1. **Review:** Type each line twice. Double space after each 2-line group.

    ```
    frf juj ftf jyj fgf jhj ded kik sws lol aqa ;p; gh
    fish joke girl quit tops glad warp quay work equal
    If Lee Quag types the work, he does it just right.
    Haste is waste.  Take it easy.  Life is too short.
    Dear Jo:  Kate says it is quite easy to type well.
    ```
    All the keys you know. Start each new line quickly.

2. **The Tabulator:** Your typewriter has a Tabulator—a device that makes the carriage move to any scale point you desire. The Tabulator has three parts: a CLEAR key, a SET key, and a TAB key. To adjust your machine for indenting, follow these steps:
    (1) Clear the machine: Remove any stops that may already be set. (A) Move carriage to right margin stop; (B) hold down the CLEAR KEY while returning carriage to left margin stop.
    (2) Set desired tab stops: Space across the paper and press SET KEY once, firmly, at each desired stopping point.
    (3) Draw carriage or move element back to left margin.
    (4) Tabulate: Move the carriage or element to each tab stop. Use the little finger on the TAB KEY.

    Flick the TAB KEY lightly with the little finger and move the finger back home.

    NOTE: If you are using a computer, check the user manual for instructions on setting tabs for the software employed.

SAMPLE MANUSCRIPT

METAMORPHOSIS--WORLD WAR I

Marc A. Lindsell
Social Studies

March 25, 19--

Using the tab key.

3. **Tabulating Practice:**
   A. Clear all tabs.
   B. Set tab stops: Pica Typewriter .... at 30, 45, and 60.
   Elite Typewriter .... at 40, 55, and 70.
   Computer .... at 3", 4.5", and 6".
   C. Type the columns horizontally—across the page.
   Tabulate: Use the Tab Key to move to columns 2, 3, and 4.

   NOTE: Column 1 begins at your left margin.

Margin	Tab Stop	Tab Stop	Tab Stop	
quip	keep	used	park	Reach for
high	quit	goes	jolt	the tab key or bar
daft	eyes	stay	with	without
sure	jury	feed	drew	looking up.
your	list	sail	work	

All the keys you know.

4. **Paragraph Typing:**
   A. Paragraphs may be single spaced or double spaced.
   B. When paragraphs are single spaced, the first word may begin at the margin, as in Example 1, or it may be indented 5 spaces, as in Example 2.
   C. When paragraphs are double spaced, the FIRST word MUST be indented 5 spaces (as in Example 3, next page).
   D. All paragraphs—single or double spaced—MUST be separated by one blank line.

EXAMPLE 1:   *Single spaced, blocked*

Good posture helps you
to type faster.

Poor posture slows your
speed and thus your skill
as a typist.

EXAMPLE 2:   *Single spaced, indented*

     Good posture helps you
to type faster.

     Poor posture slows your
speed and thus your skill as
a typist.

WORKS CITED

```
                    WORKS CITED

¹ Lindsell, Sheryl L. and Stanley L. Alpert. The Certified Professional
     Secretaries Examination. (New York: Arco Publishing, 1987), p. 123.

² Hemphill, Phyllis David. Business Communications with Writing
     Improvement Exercises. (Englewood Cliffs: Prentice Hall, 1958),
     p. 146.

³ Warriner, John and Sheila Y. Laws. English Grammar and Communication.
     (New York: Harcourt Brace Jovanovich, 1973), p. 22.

⁴ Tuckman, Bruce W. Conducting Educational Research. 2d ed. (New York:
     Harcourt Brace Jovanovich, 1978), p. 15.
```

NOTE: This is a listing of all the works that have been cited and, as aforementioned, has replaced "footnotes." All the works cited should be listed in the order in which they are indicated in the text.

WORKS CONSULTED

```
                  WORKS CONSULTED

Bailey, Thomas A., The Lusitania Disaster, New York:  The Free Press
     (division of Macmillan Publishing, Co., Inc.), 1975.

Cramer, Kenyon C., The Cause of War, Glenview, Ill.:  Scott Foresman
     and Co., 1965.

Gray, Edwyn, The Killing of Time: The U-Boat War 1914-1918, New York:
     Charles Scribner's Sons, 1972.

May, Ernest, R., The World War and American Isolation 1914-1917, Cam-
     bridge, Mass.:  Harvard University Press, 1966.

Millis, Walter, Road to War: America, 1914-1917, New York:  Howard
     Fertig, Inc., 1970.
```

The *Works Consulted* has replaced the bibliography. This is a listing of all sources of reference and starts two inches from the top of the page. It has one-inch side margins, and five additional spaces are indented for runover lines. The format is the reverse of a paragraph.

All entries are in alphabetical order by author's last name.

EXAMPLE 3: *Double-spaced, indented*

    Good posture helps you

to type faster.

    Poor posture slows your

speed and thus your skill as

a typist.

5. **Paragraph Practice:** Double Spacing.
   You get one extra word credit each time you use the Tab Key.
   A. Clear the machine.
   B. Set a tab stop 5 spaces from left margin.
   C. Set line-space regulator at ''2'' for double spacing. Double spacing shows 1 blank line between typed lines.
   D. Type each paragraph slowly, smoothly. Practice each word that has an error. Try for a PERFECT copy of each paragraph.

WORDS

        Your goal is good skill.   The way to get good   10

All the keys   skill is to work hard for it.   It is the sure way.   20
you know.   1   2   3   4   5   6   7   8   9   10

        So quit the talk.   Just work for the goal you   10

   seek.   Put forth good effort.   Reward will follow.   20
             1   2   3   4   5   6   7   8   9   10

6. **Test Your Skill:** Take Three 1-Minute Timings.
   Goal: 15 words a minute within 3 errors.
           Record your best speed within 3 errors.

            Single-Spaced, Blocked Paragraph.
            Set Line-Space Regulator at ''1.''

All the keys   Dear Walt: Go with Joel Qualey to see if that old   10
you know.   house at the edge of the park lake is still there.   20
                  1   2   3   4   5   6   7   8   9   10

Lesson 9: The Tabulator

25

TITLE PAGE

Although many styles are acceptable, the title page generally contains the title of the report; the name of the person who prepared it; the office, school, or institution from which it originated; the date on which it was presented; and, in many cases, to whom it was presented.

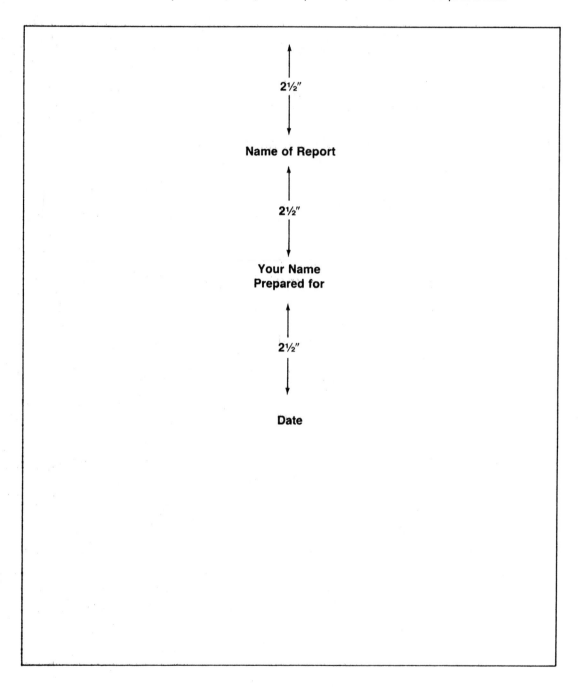

LESSON 10
NEW KEYS
C V / (Slant)

COMPUTER MARGINS: 1" (left and right)
TYPEWRITER MARGINS: 15–70 (Pica)
25–80 (Elite)
SPACING: Single

1. **Review:** Type each line twice. Double space after each 2-line group.

   ```
   frf juj ftf jyj fgf jhj ded kik sws lol aqa ;p; qp     All the keys
   word fish joke quay girl harp quit glad tops equal      you know.
   Look at your work; it tells you how well you type.
   We will offer all help to the quiet lad who works.     Space
                                                          quickly
   Judge Kurt P. Quays will free the slow jury today.     after each
                                                          word.
   ```

2. **New-Key Practice: C** *Use D-Finger.*
   Practice the reach from **D** to **C** and back home to **D**. Curl the **D**-finger as it reaches down to **C**. Keep the **A**-finger in home position. When you can reach **C** without looking at your fingers, type each line twice:

   ```
   c c c c dcd dcd dcd dcd; cut cut cut; cue cue cue;     In the word
   dcd dcd dcd cur cur cur; cud cud cud; cup cup cup;     ice, line 4,
                                                          move
   dcd dcd dcd cat cat cat; cap cap cap; cow cow cow;     D-finger
   dcd dcd dcd cod cod cod; ice ice ice; cog cog cog;     from C to E
                                                          without
   cut cap cog cry cod cow cash jack calf tack quick;     pausing on
                                                          home key.
   ```

3. **New-Key Practice: V** *Use F-Finger.*
   Practice the reach from **F** to **V** and back home to **F**. Keep the **A S D** fingers in home position. When you can reach **V** without looking at your fingers, type each line twice:

   ```
   v v v v fvf fvf fvf fvf; via via via; vow vow vow;
   fvf fvf fvf vet vet vet; vie vie vie; eve eve eve;
   fvf fvf fvf Vic Vic Vic; Val Val Val; vat vat vat;
   pave pave pave; void void void; Vicki Vicki Vicki;
   rave vows jive gave have five caves quiver voyage;
   ```

LESSON 34
MANUSCRIPT TYPING

1. Paper:
   - A. Use 8½ × 11 white bond.
   - B. Type on 1 side only.

2. Spacing:
   - A. Double space all lines.
   - B. Indent all paragraphs 5 to 7 spaces.

3. Margin Stops:
   Typewriter: 15–75 (Pica); 20–85 (Elite). Computer: 1" (left and right).

4. Top Margin—Page 1
   2 inches: 12 lines
   - A. Space down 13 single lines from top edge of the paper.
   - B. Center the title in all capitals and/or underscore.
   - C. Space down 3 single lines and start the first line in the copy.
     (If a cover page is used, steps B and C may be eliminated.)

5. Top Margin—Page 2 and following pages
   1 inch: 6 lines
   - A. Space down 7 single lines from top edge of the paper.
   - B. Continue with the text.

6. Bottom Margin:
   1 inch on all pages
   - A. Make a light pencil mark about 1½ inches from the bottom.
   - B. Type 3 more lines after reaching this mark.

7. Paragraph Headings:
   - A. Space down 3 single lines from last typewritten line.
   - B. Start the paragraph heading at the margin in all capitals.
   - C. Double space and start paragraph.

8. Quotations
   3 lines or less:
   4 lines or more:
   Type the quotation in the same paragraph—within quotation marks.
   Type the quotation in a separate blocked paragraph without quotation marks. Use short lines, single spacing.

9. Page Numbers:
   - A. Do not number the first page.
   - B. Type 2 on line 3 of second page at the right margin.

10. Works Cited a/k/a Footnotes
    Works Consulted a/k/a Bibliography
    Footnotes and bibliographies seem to be going the way of the dinosaur. According to the *MLA* [*Modern Language Association*] *Handbook for Writers of Research Papers,* footnotes are now listed at the conclusion of a paper under the heading of "Works Cited." If you are including works that have been used for research and not necessarily cited, merely include them under the heading of "Works Consulted," the new term for bibliography.

These rules are illustrated by the models on the following pages.

4. **New-Key Practice: / (Slant)** *Use ;-Finger.*
   Practice the reach from **;** to **/** and back home to **;**. Keep the **J-** and **K**-fingers in home position. When you can reach the **/**-key without looking at your fingers, type each line twice:

c/o =
care of
c/l =
car lots
s/s =
steamship

```
/ / / / ;/; ;/; ;/; c/o c/o; c/l c/l; s/s s/s s/s
;/; ;/; ;/; his/yours his/yours; we/they we/they;
```

5. **Paragraph Practice:** Double Spacing.
   A. Type each paragraph slowly, smoothly.
   B. Practice each word that has an error.
   C. Try for a PERFECT copy of each paragraph.

WORDS

Set your
line-space
regulator at
"2."

```
        Skill grows at a quiet pace.  Hurry is waste.        10
Type at such a rate that you feel at perfect ease.          20
        1     2     3     4     5     6     7     8     9     10
```

```
        Type at a very steady pace, without pauses or        10
jerks.  This is how you will develop a good skill.          20
        1     2     3     4     5     6     7     8     9     10
```

6. **Test Your Skill:** Take Three 1-Minute Timings.
   Goal: 15 words a minute within 3 errors.
   Record your best speed within 3 errors.

   Single-Spaced, Blocked Paragraph.
   Set Line-Space Regulator at "1."

All the keys
you know.

```
Dear Vicki:  Pat Garvy takes the speed test today.          10
Jud Quat is out of practice; he will try it later.          20
        1     2     3     4     5     6     7     8     9     10
```

Lesson 10: C V / (Slant)

TYPING ON LINES

In your business or personal work, you may often have to type on lines. To do so:

1. Move the variable line spacer toward you and roll the cylinder to bring the line into correct position for typing.

2. Test the position of the line: Set the ribbon control lever for stencil and tap one underscore. The light line it makes tells you whether to roll the paper up or down.

3. Reset the ribbon control lever to its original position. Then type.

   EXAMPLES: This is too high.

   This is too low.

   This is just right.

ALIGNING

Aligning is the technique of inserting omitted letters after the paper has been removed.

1. Type the alphabet on a sheet of paper:

   abcdefghijklmnopqrstuvwxyz

   Note how close the vertical white lines on YOUR aligning scale come to the center of the letters.

2. Type this name EXACTLY as shown: Geo ge Wilkins n

3. Remove the paper. Reinsert it. See that it is straight. Roll up the paper till the name is close to the aligning scale. Adjust the paper so that the white lines on the aligning scale point to the center of **i** and **l**. Use the paper release and the variable line spacer.

4. Move the carriage to the space for the **r** in Geo ge. Set ribbon control lever on stencil. Tap the **r**. The faint mark will show whether you need to make another adjustment. Return the lever to its normal position. Type the **r**. Then type the **o** in Wilkins n.

   Too high: Geo^{r}ge Wilkins^{o}n

   Too low: Geo$_r$ge Wilkins$_o$n

   Just right: George Wilkinson

5. **Practice:** A. Type each line EXACTLY as shown:

   J seph J seph J seph
   Robe t Robe t Robe t
   Wal er Wal er Wal er

   B. Remove the paper. Reinsert and align it.
   C. Type the missing **o r t**.

Lesson 33: Mastery Drills, Timed Tests, Problem Solving   **122**

LESSON 11
NEW KEYS
B M X

Line 3:
Move
D-finger
from C to E
and
F-finger
from R to V
without
pausing on
home key.

1. **Review:** Type each line twice. Double space after each 2-line group.

```
fr ju ft jy fg jh de ki sw lo aq ;p fv ;/ fv dc ;/
fist jerk cave hogs quit wade yule aqua kegs pelt;
vice vice vice slice slice slice curve curve curve
If you wish to keep a secret, keep it to yourself.
Every day is a good day if you put it to good use.
```

Try to type
each repeat
line a little
faster.

2. **New-Key Practice: B** *Use F-Finger.*
   Practice the reach from **F** to **B** and back home to **F**. Keep the **A S D** fingers in home position.
   When you can reach **B** without looking at your fingers, type each line twice:

```
b b b b fbf fbf fbf fbf; but but but; bid bid bid;
fbf fbf fbf bag bag bag; boy boy boy; bow bow bow;
fbf fbf fbf bar bar bar; bus bus bus; cub cub cub;
lab lab; bug bug bug; fob fob fob; quibble quibble
hub web big buy pub rib jab rub tub ebb bake above
```

Hit space
bar.

3. **New-Key Practice: M** *Use J-Finger.*
   Practice the reach from **J** to **M** and back home to **J**. Keep the **K L ;** fingers in home position.
   When you can reach **M** without looking at your fingers, type each line twice:

```
m m m m jmj jmj jmj jmj; mad mad mad; may may may;
jmj jmj jmj mug mug mug; mop mop mop; Mac Mac Mac;
jmj jmj jmj vim vim vim; hum hum hum; mal mal mal;
aim aim aim met met met; mow mow mow; rim rim rim;
gym mob mud gum jam sum him mar milk qualm flames;
```

Move
J-finger
from U to
M; from
M to U
without
pausing on
home key.

NAME	HOW MADE	EXAMPLE
13. Roman numerals	Type capital letters.	I V X L C D M
14. Star*	1. Type a small **v**; 2. Backspace; 3. Type a capital **A**.	✿ ✿ ✿ ✿ ✿
15. Military zero*	1. Type a regular **0**; 2. Backspace; 3. Type a slant.	Start at Ø2ØØ.
16. Brackets (Standard on most computers and typewriters.)	*Left Bracket* 1. Turn roller down 1 line and type an underscore; 2. Turn roller up 1 line and backspace twice; 3. Type a slant; 4. Backspace once and type an underscore. *Right Bracket* 1. Turn roller down 1 line and type an underscore; 2. Turn roller up 1 line and backspace once; 3. Type a slant; 4. Backspace twice and type an underscore.	She ⌐/ Pat Hix_/
17. Bar graph line	Type small **m** in a solid row.	mmmmmmmmmmmmmm
18. Fractions not on keyboard	1. Type number and slant. 2. Space after the whole number if fraction is made. 3. Do not space after the whole number if fraction is on keyboard. 4. If one fraction in a sentence is made, all of them must be made.	3/4, 5/6, 7/9 3 4/5, 10 3/7 2¼, 10½, 125½ 2/3, 1/4, 1/2

*NOTE: These procedures cannot be done on a computer because you can only place one character in a space.

Lesson 33: Mastery Drills, Timed Tests, Problem Solving

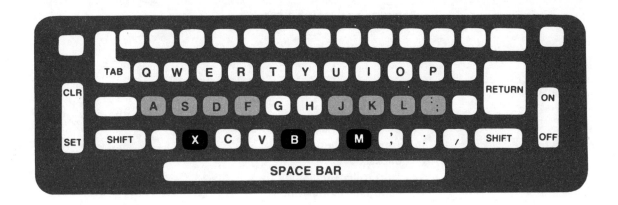

4. **New-Key Practice: X** *Use S-Finger.*
   Practice the reach from **S** to **X** and back home to **S**. Curl the **S**-finger as it reaches to **X**. Keep the **F**-finger in home position. When you can reach **X** without looking at your fingers, type each line twice:

```
x x x x sxs sxs sxs sxs; six six six; tax tax tax;    Hold hands
sxs sxs sxs box box box; lax lax lax; wax wax wax;    parallel to
pox pox pox vex vex vex; hex hex hex; axe axe axe;    the slant
fox fox fox Dix Dix Dix; Cox Cox Cox; Rex Rex Rex;    of the
sex mix axe wax pox lax fox hex box flux Max Xmas;    keyboard.
```

5. **Paragraph Practice:**
   Try for a PERFECT copy of each paragraph.

   WORDS

```
     Aim to excel.  Do your daily task to the best     10
of your ability.  Good work leads to a happy life.     20
Remember:  Success comes if you strive quite hard.     30
     1     2     3     4     5     6     7     8     9     10
```

```
     To develop a skill takes time, of course.  So     10
devote as much time as possible to your daily work     20
here.  Have faith.  Expert skill will come to you.     30
     1     2     3     4     5     6     7     8     9     10
```

6. **Test Your Skill:** Take Three 1-Minute Timings.
   Goal: 15 words a minute within 3 errors.
   Record your best speed within 3 errors.

   Single-Spaced, Blocked Paragraph.
   Set Line-Space Regulator at "1."

   WORDS

```
All the keys   Dear Paul:  Jack said he will meet you at the ball     10
you know.      game Friday.  Vic Quay will take you home by taxi.     20
               1     2     3     4     5     6     7     8     9     10
```

SPECIAL SYMBOLS

NAME	HOW MADE	EXAMPLE
1. Times or By sign	Type a small **x**.	What is 7 x 9? a 10 x 15 rug
2. Equal sign	1. Type a hyphen; 2. Backspace; 3. Turn roller up slightly by hand and type hyphen again. (Some machines have the = key.)	10 x 10 = 100
3. Plus sign (Standard on most computers.)	1. Type a hyphen; 2. Backspace; 3. Type a slant. (Some machines have the + key.)	90 ≠ 10 = 100
4. Minus sign	Type a hyphen.	100 − 10 = 90
5. Division sign	1. Type a hyphen; 2. Backspace; 3. Type a colon.	100 ÷ 10 = 10
6. Degree sign	Turn roller down slightly by hand and type a small **o**.	Temperature 9°
7. Raised number (Superscript on many computers.)	Turn roller down slightly by hand and type the number.	$x^2 - y^3 - xy^3$
8. Lowered number	Turn roller slightly up by hand and type the number.	H_2O is water.
9. Feet and inches (after numbers)	Apostrophe for feet. Quotation mark for inches.	Length is 10' Length is 10"
10. Minutes, seconds (after numbers)	Apostrophe for minutes. Quotation mark for seconds.	Maxie ran the mile in 5' 3".
11. Caret	1. Type an underscore and a slant; 2. Center the inserted word above the slant.	the Hy mad_e/ team.
12. Pounds* (British money)	1. Type a small **f**; 2. Backspace; 3. Type a capital **L**.	Price is £10

Lesson 33: Mastery Drills, Timed Tests, Problem Solving

LESSON 12
NEW KEYS
Z N ?

COMPUTER MARGINS: 1" (left and right)
TYPEWRITER MARGINS: 15–70 (Pica)
                        25–80 (Elite)
SPACING: Single

1. **Review:** Type each line twice. Double space after each 2-line group.

Line 4:
Move
F-finger
from R to
B; from B
to T without
pausing on
home key.

```
abcd efgh ijkl mopq rstu vwxy abcd efgh ijkl mopq;
ark how eve box sue fly pad two hum jigs quit deck
A small boy with a watch has the time of his life.
verb verb verb curbs curbs curbs debts debts debts
much much much jumps jumps jumps rumor rumor rumor
```

Line 5:
Move
J-finger
from M to
U; from
U to M
without
pausing on
home key.

2. **New-Key Practice: Z** *Use A-Finger.*
   Practice the reach from **A** to **Z** and back home to **A**. Curl the finger as it reaches down to **Z**. Keep the **F**-finger in home position. When you can reach **Z** without looking at your fingers, type each line twice:

```
z z z z aza aza aza aza; zig zig zig; zag zag zag;
aza aza aza zip zip zip; zoo zoo zoo; zed zed zed;
aza aza aza adz adz adz; fiz fiz fiz; amaze amaze;
blitz blitz blitz; tizzy tizzy tizzy; craze craze;
viz., zest jazz lazy Zeke quiz whizz zebra zephyr;
```

Fix each
key location
in your
mind.

3. **New-Key Practice: N** *Use J-Finger.*
   Practice the reach from **J** to **N** and back home to **J**. Keep the **K L ;** fingers in home position. When you can reach **N** without looking at your fingers, type each line twice:

All the
alphabet
keys.

```
n n n n jnj jnj jnj jnj; nil nil nil; sun sun sun;
jnj jnj jnj Ben Ben Ben; run run run; can can can;
jnj jnj jnj van van van; end end end; nix nix nix;
pen pen pen gun gun gun; now now now; ton ton ton;
won yen fun man gun hun din zinc junk links queen;
```

Move
J-finger
from U to
N; from
N to U
without
pausing on
home key.

COMMON ERRORS IN MACHINE OPERATION

ERROR	CAUSE	REMEDY
1. Raised Capitals	Releasing shift key too soon.	Hold shift key down till you have typed the capital letter.
2. Blurred Letters	Not releasing the keys instantly.	Lightly tap and release the keys.
3. Uneven Left Margin	Returning the carriage weakly, or with too much force.	Move "pinky" to RETURN key and wait till the carriage stops.
4. Omission or Insertion of Words	Looking up from the copy, causing you to lose the place.	Keep your eyes on the copy all the time. Use will power.
5. Uneven Indenting	Not holding the tab key down until carriage has stopped.	Hold the tab key down firmly until carriage has stopped.
6. Overlapping Letters and Spaces	Typing jerkily, causing strokes to miss their normal spacing.	Type evenly, smoothly, at a steady pace. Do not rush.
7. Omission of Space or Leaving an Extra Space	Probably holding your thumb on space bar, or leaning your palm on machine.	Hold thumb ½ inch above space bar and wrists ½ inch above machine. Bounce thumb off space bar. Keep palms off machine.
8. Reversing Letters	Reading too far ahead of your typing.	Fix eyes on the copy. If necessary, spell the words to yourself.
9. Double Impressions	Pushing or pounding the keys.	Tap keys lightly.

Lesson 33: Mastery Drills, Timed Tests, Problem Solving　　　　　　　　**119**

4. **New-Key Practice: ?** *Use ;-Finger.*

The **?** is on the /-key. Practice the reach like this: (1) Depress left shift key; (2) Reach for the /-key; (3) Move fingers back home. When you can do these 3 steps smoothly without looking at your fingers, type each line twice:

```
? ? ;?; ;?; ;?; Who? Who? Why? Why? Ben? Max? Vic?
Where is Zoel?  Where is Marvin?  Where is Robert?
```
Space twice after ? at end of a sentence.

5. **Paragraph Practice:** Double Spaced.
Try for a PERFECT copy of each paragraph.

WORDS

All the alphabet keys.
```
        You want to do well in some subject.  Why not     10
perfect your typing skill?  You can use your skill        20
in many small ways to help you in your daily work.        30
        1    2    3    4    5    6    7    8    9    10
```

```
        You can also use your typing skill as a means     10
of securing an office job.  It is a valuable skill        20
to have.  You can acquire it; exert a bit of zeal.        30
        1    2    3    4    5    6    7    8    9    10
```

6. **Test Your Skill.** Take Three 1-Minute Timings.
Goal: 15 words a minute within 3 errors.
Record your best speed within 3 errors.

Single-Spaced, Blocked Paragraph.
Set Line-Space Regulator at "1."

WORDS

All the alphabet keys.
```
Mr. Querz:  Joel Knox will get the xerox copies by     10
Tuesday.  You will have five samples the same day.     20
        1    2    3    4    5    6    7    8    9    10
```

If you go into a store and buy things without 10
paying cash for them, you are said to be buying on 20
credit; that is, in lieu of paying cash you pledge 30
to pay for the goods at some future time. A great 40
many big firms do business on an all—credit basis. 50

The free use of credit has grown into an im- 60
portant factor in our business life today. It is 70
said that the folks who buy on credit in our land 80
now owe many billions of dollars for things which 90
they bought on time, or for money which they have 100
borrowed. About a third of the money owed is for 110
these goods: cars, radios, TV sets, and furniture. 120

Why has credit been used so much in our busi- 130
ness life? It is thought that most folks who buy 140
on credit see in credit the only way they can get 150
all the goods they desire but cannot pay in cash. 160

1   2   3   4   5   6   7   8   9   10

The choice of a career is not an easy matter. 10
Tests cannot give a positive answer concerning the 20
career you should choose. You are too complex for 30
accurate and complete analysis. A test that shows 40
you are capable of doing a certain type of work is 50
no proof that you will be happy doing it. For the 60
choice of a career depends on a variety of factors. 70

The most important factors are your likes and 80
dislikes. So it seems you have to choose your own 90
career. No one can make the choice for you. Your 100
need for ready money might force you to accept the 110
first job offered. Such necessity should not kill 120
your drive to seek the kind of job you are set on. 130
You can still climb your way, little by little, to 140
that job. Make sure your choice is an intelligent 150
one. Then equip yourself for that sort of career. 160

1   2   3   4   5   6   7   8   9   10

LESSON 13
NEW KEYS
- (Hyphen) Shift Lock

COMPUTER MARGINS: 1" (left and right)
TYPEWRITER MARGINS: 15–70 (Pica)
25–80 (Elite)
SPACING: Single

1. **Review:** Type each line twice. Double space after each 2-line group. The last line is easy. Practice it several times for speed. Start slowly, then g-r-a-d-u-a-l-l-y pick up speed as you go.

Home Row:	`ask jal; ask a lad; half a glass; a lad had a fall`	Keep wrists
First Row:	`lax lax van van max max can can cab cabs jazz jazz`	low and
Third Row:	`wit yet ire ore type quit wrote erupt witty puppet`	relaxed but
Alphabet:	`The quick brown fox jumped over the lazy old dogs.`	off the typewriter
Speedup:	`You can do the work well if you know how to do it.`	frame.

```
    1     2     3     4     5     6     7     8     9    10
```

2. **New-Key Practice: - (Hyphen)** *Use ;-Finger.*
Practice the reach from semicolon to hyphen and back home to semicolon. Straighten the ;-finger as it goes up for the hyphen. Keep the **J**-finger in home position. When you can reach the hyphen without looking at your fingers, type each line twice:

All the alphabet keys.

```
- - - ;-; ;-; ;-; ;-; one-half; one-half; one-half
;-; ;-; one-fifth; one-sixth; blue-gray; all-black
;-; ;-; zig-zag; part-time; half-price; by-product
;-; ;-; second-rate; son-in-law; up-to-date jacket
ice-clad; ready-made; quick-witted; vice-president
```

No space before or after a hyphen.

3. **New-Key Practice: Shift Lock**
The Shift Lock is above one or both of the shift keys. Use it to type a word or group of words in CAPITALS.

For the left shift lock .... use the **A**-finger.
For the right shift lock .... use the **;**-finger.

(1) Press the shitt lock; move the finger home.
(2) Type the word or words.
(3) Release the lock by tapping the opposite shift key.

A MAGIC TRICK

Do you enjoy magic tricks? Here is one trick	10
you will enjoy trying out on some of your friends:	20
Ask the friend to jot down his age on a piece	30
of paper; then say that you will guess his correct	40
age if he will do as follows: Multiply the number	50
by two and add four to the answer. Then, multiply	60
by three and divide by six. Ask to see the number	70
your friend now has. Subtract two from the number	80
and you will then tell the person his correct age.	90
Example: The person's age is 19. Ask him or	100
her to multiply it by 2; that makes it 38; 38 plus	110
4 is 42; 42 times 3 is 126; 126 divided by 6 is 21;	120
21 minus 2 is age 19. Try to memorize these steps	130
exactly. It would spoil the fun to read them from	140
a memo. The trick works with any number selected.	150

```
1     2     3     4     5     6     7     8     9     10
```

HOW TO READ FASTER

Anyone who can read can learn to read faster.	10
You do not need a keen mind for reading speed. An	20
education helps but if you have a fairly large vo-	30
cabulary, you really do not need formal education.	40
The slow readers have a habit of reading word	50
by word; they devote full attention to every word.	60
They should, instead, look only for the meaning of	70
groups of words. What you really want in all your	80
reading is the author's idea. The words he or she	90
uses are not important. Many words can be cut out	100
of a piece of writing without loss of the meaning.	110
So get the habit of reading solely for ideas.	120
You will then see that you are taking in groups of	130
words at a glance and that you are reading faster.	140
To help you keep in mind what you read, train your	150
mind to see the way the author presents the ideas.	160

```
1     2     3     4     5     6     7     8     9     10
```

Type each line twice.

All the alphabet keys.

To type words in ALL CAPITALS, use the SHIFT LOCK.
Zoel Buxton is now typing SMOOTHLY and ACCURATELY.
Dear Jacqueline: Who types FASTER, Max or Victor?
See the expert BOUNCE his THUMB off the space bar.
DEXTERITY in any skill comes from PROPER PRACTICE.

Release the shift lock instantly after you have typed the word or words in ALL CAPITALS.

4. **Paragraph Practice:** Single-Spaced, Blocked.
   Try for a PERFECT copy of each paragraph:

   Dear Joe: Do you happen to know how far the equa-
   tor is from Houston, Texas? What do you estimate?
       1   2   3   4   5   6   7   8   9   10

Hyphen used to divide a word at end of a line.

All the alphabet keys.

   Dear Vera: I am glad to hear that your sister-in-
   law passed the examination for high school teacher.
       1   2   3   4   5   6   7   8   9   10

Hyphen used to combine words into a "compound" word.

   Dear Buzz: Did you know that Roxie Jimson--Shorty
   to the class--won that school typewriting contest?
       1   2   3   4   5   6   7   8   9   10

2 hyphens used for a dash. No space before or after a dash.

5. **Test Your Skill:** Take Three 1-Minute Timings.
   Goal: 15 words a minute within 3 errors.
       Record your best speed within 3 errors.

WORDS

   You can get there faster with push than with pull.   10
   Time is money; so you must put it to the best use.   20
       1   2   3   4   5   6   7   8   9   10

	WORDS
Be a better typist--follow these suggestions:	10
First, correct technique at the machine--sit erect	20
as tall as you can, feet flat on floor, eyes fixed	30
on the copy. Snap all keys on the manual machine;	40
tap them very lightly on the electric. Return the	50
carriage quickly, with eyes held on the copy. Be-	60
gin each line without pausing--without looking up.	70
Second, keep your mind only on the matter you	80
are typing. Pass quickly from word to word but do	90
not read ahead. Just type at an even, steady pace	100
without jerks. This way you develop accuracy plus	110
speed--the two basic elements of competent typing.	120
Third, learn to use every labor-saving device	130
on your machine just as the expert does--by touch.	140

   1   2   3   4   5   6   7   8   9   10

THE STORY OF KING MIDAS

	WORDS
In olden times, long, long ago, there lived a	10
king named Midas. He lived in a beautiful palace.	20
He had a pretty wife and a pretty daughter whom he	30
dearly loved, and lots of money to buy everything.	40
Yet this king was not happy. He was a miser.	50
He loved money for its own sake. In a secret room	60
in his palace he kept all his gold. He spent each	70
day counting over and over again his golden hoard.	80
One day he asked the Greek god named Dionysus	90
to grant him the wish of his life--that everything	100
he touched might turn to gold; and it was granted.	110
But King Midas, when he saw even his food changed	120
to gold, had to beg the god to take his gift back.	130
The story of King Midas is a myth, a fanciful	140
tale that has come down to us from many ages past.	150

   1   2   3   4   5   6   7   8   9   10

LESSON 14
MARGIN RELEASE

COMPUTER MARGINS: 1" (left and right)
TYPEWRITER MARGINS: 15–70 (Pica)
                        25–80 (Elite)
SPACING: Single

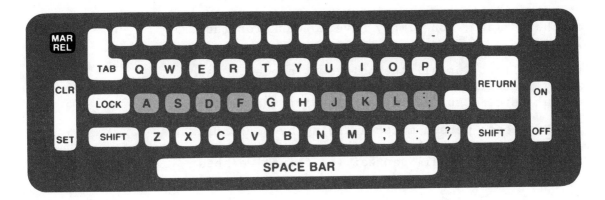

1. **Review:** Type each line twice. Double space after each 2-line group.

Alphabet: feed back soap high flux over quit jazz many words
    Shift: Lee Cal Moe Vic Pat Gil Ike Eve Ray Nora Walt Hugh
       A: and aid ale; ant all air; apt ace ark; act age aim
       B: bit boy but; beg bid bow; box bar bib; beg bin bob
  Speedup: The man who did not do the work will not get paid.
            1   2   3   4   5   6   7   8   9   10

Stretch shift-key finger. Keep other fingers in typing position.

2. **Paragraph Practice:**
    A. Type each paragraph twice—slowly, smoothly.
    B. Practice each word that has an error.
    C. Try for a PERFECT copy of each paragraph.

WORDS

You are now able to type by touch. This means   10
that you can type--without looking at your fingers.   20
1   2   3   4   5   6   7   8   9   10

The more you type by touch, the faster you can   10
type. Soon, you will be a rapid, competent typist.   20
1   2   3   4   5   6   7   8   9   10

You will have a highly valuable skill that you   10
can put to use in your personal and business tasks.   20
1   2   3   4   5   6   7   8   9   10

NOTE: If you are using a computer, check the user's manual for instructions on setting margins for the software used.

WORKING FOR A LIVING

You want a place in which to live, the proper	10
food, clothing, and all the other things that make	20
for comfort and convenience and life worth living.	30
But all the things you desire you cannot have just	40
for the asking. You simply have to work for them.	50
Yet, at one time each family had to depend on	60
its own effort for all the things it needed. Each	70
family made its own clothing, raised its own food,	80
and put aside a sufficient surplus for the winter.	90
Now, each person makes a living by performing	100
special work for which he or she is paid in money.	110
With this money we all can get the things we need.	120

      1   2   3   4   5   6   7   8   9   10

CARE OF THE TYPEWRITER

Your typewriter will give you good service if	10
you take good care of it. Good care avoids costly	20
repairs and gives your machine a much longer life.	30
Here are a few things to do every day to keep	40
your machine working at top efficiency: Clean the	50
ink and grime from type bars with a bristle brush.	60
Clean other parts with the long-handled typewriter	70
brush. Wipe upper and lower parts of the carriage	80
rail with a cloth. Remove dust from under machine.	90
Cover the machine when you have finished your work.	100
Once a week clean the type with type cleaner.	110
Clean cylinder and feed rolls with denatured alco-	120
hol. Spread a drop or two of oil on carriage rail.	130

      1   2   3   4   5   6   7   8   9   10

Lesson 33: Mastery Drills, Timed Tests, Problem Solving

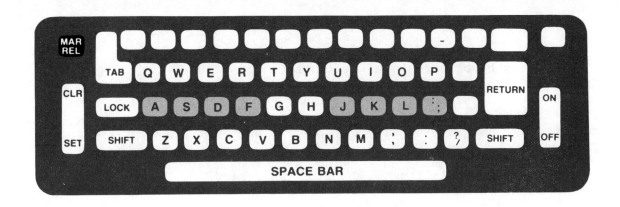

3. **Margin Release:** Sometimes you may find it necessary to type a few letters beyond your right margin stop. For example: In paragraph 3-A below, the lines extend beyond 70 (Pica); 80 (Elite). So when you hear the margin bell:
   (1) Type on until the keys lock.
   (2) Press Margin Release key at top of keyboard, right or left.
   (3) Finish typing the line.

   Practice: Type 2 copies of paragraph 3-A.

3-A.

Double
Spacing.
      The many different makes and models of typewriters have

different means of setting margin stops. Study your machine

to determine how to adjust the stops quickly like an expert.

4. **Test Your Skill:** Take Three 1-Minute Timings.
   Goal: 15 words a minute within 3 errors.
         Record your best speed within 3 errors.

WORDS

All the
alphabet
keys.
      Paul visited Rex and Zolie when they got back   10

from Japan and Iraq and heard about their voyages.   20

    1   2   3   4   5   6   7   8   9   10

NOTE: If you are using a computer, you won't need a margin release. Your text will automatically wrap to the next line.

You may have heard about Diogenes, a wise man   10
of ancient Greece. On one occasion he walked down   20
many streets of his home town at midday carrying a   30
lighted lantern. When he was asked to account for   40
such strange conduct, he said that he was out just   50
looking for an honest man.   55

Folks started to laugh and shake their heads.   65
They thought there was surely something wrong with   75
him. But, of course, we all now know he was sane.   85
He simply tried to dramatize the fact that honesty   95
in his day was a rare virtue. Even now in our own   105
day and age it seems this virtue is not yet common.   115

  1   2   3   4   5   6   7   8   9   10

Money's the best gift; it's easy to exchange.   10
The love of money is a love which never grows old.   20
Money is what you use if you have no credit cards.   30
The trouble with money is that it favors the rich.   40

Anybody with cold cash gets a warm reception.   50
What gives money its value is the work you put in.   60
Some folks never think of money—when they owe it.   70
Money talks but it does so only with the very few.   80

Money will be our best friend in our old age.   90
Money makes the car go and the car makes money go.   100
Money is mighty but can't make a dog wag its tail.   110
A dollar would go farther if it didn't go so fast.   120

  1   2   3   4   5   6   7   8   9   10

Lesson 33: Mastery Drills, Timed Tests, Problem Solving

LESSON 15
NEW KEYS
1 3 7

1. **Review:** Type each line twice. Double space after each 2-line group.

Alphabet: abc cde efg ghi ijk klm mno opq qrs stu uvwx xyzab
C: cot cub cab; cop cow cur; cat can cup; cob coy cad
D: did due dad; dip die dab; day din dye; dew dun dog
(Hyphen): ;-; ;-; ;-; zig-zag; re-enter; part-time; one-half
Speedup: Why did we not pay that man who did all that work?
          1   2   3   4   5   6   7   8   9   10

2. **New-Key Practice: 1**
   If you have a **1** key on top row, use **A**-finger.
   If you have no **1** key, type the small **L** for **1.**
   Type each line twice:

   ala ala ala ala Add 1 and 1 and 11 and 11 and 111.   Relax your
   11 acts 11 apes 11 axes 11 lads 11 loads 11 lamps;   shoulders.
   Cal will be 1 year and 11 months old next June 11.   Let your
   We need 11 pairs of size 11 socks for the 11 boys.   arms hang
   Bus No. 11 on Route 11 is due to arrive in 1 hour.   loosely at
                                                        your sides.

3. **New-Key Practice: 3** *Use D-Finger.*
   Practice the reach from **D** to **3** and back home to **D**. Keep the **F**-finger at home. When
   you can reach **3** without looking at your fingers, type each line twice:

   3 3 3 d3d d3d d3d 3 and 31 and 113 and 131 and 313   Think the
   3 days 3 dogs 3 dads; 33 dolls 33 dishes 33 dukes;   finger and
   Donald and his 3 pals caught 13 fish on August 31.   the number
   For the next quiz, read pages 3, 13, 31, 131, 133.   it controls.
   Ben Cox will be 13 years 3 months old December 31.

NOTE: Many computers feature a 10-key numeric pad, affording you the ability to enter numeric
       information at high speeds. This is especially useful to a person who is accustomed to
       performing numeric calculations on a calculator. If you would like to practice on the
       10-key numeric pad, SIMPLIFIED KEYBOARDING FOR DATA ENTRY, by Sheryl Lind-
       sell-Roberts, is available through Arco Publishing, offering a variety of exercises.

5-MINUTE TIMED TESTS
(Pages 114 to 118)

Before You Take a Test:

1. Clear the machine.
2. Set margins stops: typewriter—15–70 (Pica); 25–80 (Elite); computer—1" (left and right).
3. Set line-space regulator for double spacing.

Test Procedure: (Take one test a day.)

1. Start with Test 1. Take three 5-minute timings. Repeat if you finish before end of 5 minutes.
2. After each timing, jot down total words typed and total errors.
3. Practice the words that have errors till they are easy for you.
4. Select your best speed within 5 errors.

Score Your Tests:

1. Use the Progress Chart for Timings on page 153.
2. Set your goal: 5 words a minute higher than your present speed.
3. Record your best speed in Test 1. With Test 2, start joining the scores and watch your progress.
4. If you reach your goal before Test 10, set a new goal at 5 words a minute higher than before. Start over again with Test 1.

Skill-Booster Tips:

1. Curve fingers slightly; hold them as close as possible to home keys without touching the keys. Tap the keys very lightly.
2. Move the fingers only. Try not to move wrists, elbows, arms.
3. Keep your eyes on the copy at all times.
4. Return the carriage without looking up. Begin a new line quickly.
5. Speed up the shift-key stroke. Do it in a continuous 1-2-3 motion: ONE, depress shift key. TWO, hold it down while you strike the correct key. THREE, release shift key, move finger back home.
6. Type evenly, smoothly; keep the carriage moving.
7. Type short, common words like *the, had,* without spelling them (t h e) (h a d). Flash them as a unit (the) (had).
8. Fix your mind only on the work you are doing.
9. To help you avoid frequent errors on certain letters, figures, or symbols, practice the appropriate Mastery Drills on pages 109 and 110.

4. **New-Key Practice: 7** *Use J-Finger.*
Practice the reach from **J** to **7** and back home to **J**. Keep the semicolon-finger at home. When you can reach **7** without looking at your fingers, type each line twice:

```
7 7 7 j7j j7j j7j 7 and 17 and 37 and 173 and 317;   Stretch
7 jugs 7 jars 7 jewels 17 jeeps 37 jokes 137 jobs;    finger to a
17 John Street; 37 James Avenue; 137 Jackson Blvd.    top-row
Of the 37 students, 17 typed at 13 words a minute.    key.
What is the sum of 1 and 7 and 13 and 173 and 371?
```

5. **Paragraph Practice:** Double Spacing.
Try for 2 PERFECT copies of this paragraph:

WORDS

```
    It is easy to type the figures 1 and 3 and 7.        10

It is even easy to mix these figures and type such      20

numbers as 317, 173, 371, 713, 137, 171, 737, 373.      30
    1     2     3     4     5     6     7     8     9    10
```

6. **Test Your Skill:** Take Three 2-Minute Timings.

Follow these steps in all your 2-minute timings.

A. Repeat if you finish before end of 2 minutes.
B. After each timing, jot down total words typed and total errors. Practice the words that have errors till they are easy for you.
C. Your 2-minute speed is words typed divided by 2.

EXAMPLE: 23 words ÷ 2 = 11½ = 12 words a minute.

D. Record on your Progress Chart (page 153) your best speed within 4 errors.
Goal: 18 words a minute within 4 errors.

WORDS

```
    Fix your mind on what you are typing.  Start        10

at a slow pace and gradually work up to your best        20

speed.  Do not type so fast that you lose control.       30

Typing speed grows like a baby--slowly, gradually.       40
    1     2     3     4     5     6     7     8     9    10
```

Lesson 15: 1 3 7

SPEED BOOSTERS

MARGINS: 15–70 (Pica)
25–80 (Elite)

One good way to boost your speed is to type easy sentences over and over. They help you type smoothly without pausing.

Practice each sentence till you can type it PERFECTLY in the time you select. Your words-per-minute speed is given under that time.

Time in Seconds:	15	30	45	60
Words-per-Minute:	40	20	13	10

WORDS: 1   2   3   4   5   6   7   8   9   10

1. Try to do your work just as well as you can do it.
2. Many a true word is said in jest; also many a lie.
3. Aim for the top; it may help you to land half way.
4. Mama and papa must be fit for a baby to live with.
5. In days of yore they who did not work did not eat.
6. They who type well find it easy to get a good job.
7. You must hand it to the tax man or he may take it.
8. The boss will find out if you do good work or not.
9. A man with a bald head is one who came out on top.
10. If at the end of the rope, tie a knot and hang on.
11. Your car is out of date as soon as it is paid for.
12. The law of life: You must work for what you wish.
13. If you skip a meal, you are sure to eat with zest.
14. Know your job; that is the way to make good at it.
15. Life is a game; play to win--and ever with a grin.
16. All can take a day off but no one can put it back.
17. Eat it all but chew each bite ere you let it fall.
18. Guys who do not win fair lady know not how to woo.
19. Most all men are good--as good as they have to be.
20. All work and no play robs one of some fun in life.

    1   2   3   4   5   6   7   8   9   10

LESSON 16
NEW KEYS
2 6

COMPUTER MARGINS: 1" (left and right)
TYPEWRITER MARGINS: 15–70 (Pica)
25–80 (Elite)
SPACING: Single

1. **Review:** Type each line twice. Double space after each 2-line group.

Alphabet: The quiz Jay picked for six big men will vex them.
1 3 7: Type these numbers: · 13 17 71 137 317 ·373 713 173.
E: end ere egg; eel eke ebb; elk eve eat; ewe elf eye
One-Hand: red lip wed; hip get mop; cat pin sew; hum tax kin
Speedup: The man will be paid if he fills out the pay form.

    1   2   3   4   5   6   7   8   9   10

Return to the margin quickly without looking up.

2. **New-Key Practice: 2** *Use S-Finger.*
Practice the reach from **S** to **2** and back home to **S**. Try to keep the **F**-finger in home position. When you can reach **2** without looking at your fingers, type each line twice:

2 2 2 s2s s2s s2s 2 steps 2 seals 2 shops 2 stones
2 ships 2 sails 2 sizes 2 skirts 2 shapes 2 spaces
June 27, 1232; September 12, 1272; August 23, 1322
Cora Dix will be 12 years 2 months old January 27.
Add these figures: 2, 12, 21, 23, 27, 32, and 72.

Space twice after a colon.

3. **New-Key Practice: 6** *Use J-Finger.*
Practice the reach from **J** to **6** and back home to **J**. Stretch the **J**-finger up and to the left. Keep the **;**-finger home. When you can reach **6** without looking at your fingers, type each line twice:

6 6 6 j6j j6j j6j 6 jumps 6 jails 6 jeeps 6 jests;
6 jades 6 jaunts 6 jacks 6 juries 6 jewels 6 jobs;
August 6, 1627; October 3, 1632; November 12, 1766
What is the sum of 21 and 63 and 27 and 16 and 26?
Maxie paid 62 cents for 16 stamps he used June 26.

ALPHABETIC SENTENCES

Alphabetic sentences give you a thorough review of all the letters; they help you to gain perfect control of the keyboard. Type them at an even, steady pace, as accurately as you can.

Follow this routine:

1. Try a sentence a day—type it 10 times.
2. Practice the words that have errors.
3. Type the sentence 10 more times.
4. Start over when you have done them all.

WORDS: 1   2   3   4   5   6   7   8   9   10   11   12

1. Jerry and Martha packed five dozen quilts in two huge boxes.
2. Felix Quope and Zeb Graves may cause a fire with their junk.
3. A showy trapeze artist quickly jumped over five green boxes.
4. That quip lazy Dick made about Jackie vexed a few neighbors.
5. Jack Pahlevy of Iraq found two big azure boxes of marijuana.
6. Jovial chemist Grub quickly froze a mixture of brown powder.
7. A lazy witness from Quebec vexed patient judge Walter Kache.
8. Jacqueline Wytbok purchased several fur rugs in mixed sizes.
9. Two big foxes quickly jumped over those lazy, sleeping dogs.
10. Paul Van Weems, an expert glazier, quickly finished the job.
11. The hazard of quack medicines will be exposed by Dr. Juvtig.
12. Cy Jexon, a brainy wag, quickly solved the fish maze puzzle.
13. They quizzed four experts about knowledge of juvenile crime.
14. Macy will pack my box with five dozen jugs of liquid veneer.
15. Hy Quiveg will systematize complex jobs and jack up profits.
16. Marvin quickly packed the box with five dozen jugs for Iraq.
17. Many extra quick flights to Brazil uncovered perfect jewels.
18. Cy and Elza did mix the big jar of soapy water very quickly.
19. Five pale gray taxis whizzed by the Jonquin Steamship docks.
20. Max Vidjub zips fingers quickly across keys without pausing.

     1   2   3   4   5   6   7   8   9   10   11   12

Lesson 33: Mastery Drills, Timed Tests, Problem Solving   111

4. **Paragraph Practice:** Double Spacing.
   Try for a PERFECT copy of each paragraph:

WORDS

One space
between a
whole
number and
a "made"
fraction.

  You can make any fraction that is not on your   10
keyboard by typing the /. For example: 2/3, 1/6,   20
6/7, 1/3, 3/16, 2 1/7, 6 2/3, 3 6/7, 2 1/6, 7 1/12   30

  1 2 3 4 5 6 7 8 9 10

  Business typists use the / to shorten certain   10
terms in invoices. For example, they type B/L for   20
Bill of Lading; A/C for Account; N/C for No Charge   30

  1 2 3 4 5 6 7 8 9 10

All the
alphabet
keys plus
all the
numbers
you know.

  Maxie, Buzz, and Vicki read pages 26, 31, and   10
62; they worked out problems 2, 6, 37, and 62 just   20
in time to hand them to Prof. Quimby before class.   30
Maxie, Buzz, and Vicki are pals and work together.   40

  1 2 3 4 5 6 7 8 9 10

5. **Test Your Skill:** Take Three 2-Minute Timings.
   Goal: 18 words a minute within 4 errors.
      Record your best speed within 4 errors.

WORDS

Use double
spacing.

  If you type well, you can put your ideas down   10
on paper just as fast as they pop up in your mind.   20
You will gain this goal if you put forth your best   30
efforts in your daily lesson. Learn to type well.   40

  1 2 3 4 5 6 7 8 9 10

Number Keys

1	ala ala ala aql aql 1 lass 1 light 1 apple 1 quart
2	sw2 sw2 s2s s2s s2s 2 sets 2 sales 2 sacks 2 ships
3	de3 de3 d3d d3d d3d 3 dads 3 deals 3 dukes 3 drugs
4	fr4 fr4 f4f f4f f4f 4 furs 4 firms 4 flags 4 fires
5	fr5 fr5 f5f f5f f5f 5 feet 5 fines 5 files 5 farms
6	jy6 jy6 j6j j6j j6j 6 jobs 6 jeeps 6 jokes 6 jails
7	ju7 ju7 j7j j7j j7j 7 jugs 7 jumps 7 jokes 7 jacks
8	ki8 ki8 k8k k8k k8k 8 kits 8 kinds 8 kicks 8 kites
9	lo9 lo9 l9l l9l l9l 9 lads 9 lamps 9 lives 9 locks
10	;p0 ;p0 ;0; ;0; ;0; 10 pay 10 put 10 pals 10 pints

Symbol/Special Keys

$	f$f f$f f$f f$f Give her $40 or $41 or $42 or $43.
&	j&j j&j j&j j&j Macy & Web; Zale & Quig; Dix & Co.
%	f%f f%f f%f f%f I got 25%; Cy got 35%; Al got 40%.
#	d#d d#d d#d d#d We need 73# of #38 and 63# of #39.
( )	l(l l(l ;); ;); (one) (two) (three) (four) (five);
:	;:; ;:; ;:; Dear Al: Dear Hy: Dear Jo: Dear Ma:
?	;?; ;?; ;?; He? Who? Why? When? Which? Where?
/	;/; ;/; ;/; a/c d/c n/c c/o and/or we/they 2/3 5/8
½	;½; ;½; ;½; ½ of 60; ½ of 128; ½ of 394; ½ of 576;
¼	;¼; ;¼; ;¼; ¼ of 56; ¼ of 218; ¼ of 390; ¼ of 475;

Practice the following drills.

—	j—j j—j j—j j—j We <u>must</u> have <u>all the copies</u> today.
	;—; ;—; ;—; ;—; Your money is <u>refunded</u> in <u>10 days</u>.
¢	;¢; ;¢; ;¢; ;¢; pops 10¢; candies 20¢; franks 30¢;
	j¢j j¢j j¢j j¢j caps 26¢; horns 36¢; balloons 46¢;
@	;@; ;@; ;@; bags @ 20¢; boxes @ 30¢; cartons @ 90¢
	s@s s@s s@s bags @ 23¢; boxes @ 25¢; cartons @ 28¢
"	s"s s"s s"s s"s "wow" "sow" "slow" "show" "straw";
	;"; ;"; ;"; ;"; "pep" "pup" "plop" "prop" "plump";
'	k'k k'k k'k Dick's coat; Dick's scarf; Dick's pin;
	;'; ;'; ;'; Hap's tires; Hap's auto; Hap's garage;
*	;*; ;*; ;*; ;*; Sale lots are marked *; as 10* 20* 30*
	k*k k*k k*k k*k Sale lots are marked *; as 48* 58* 68*

LESSON 17
NEW KEYS
5 9

COMPUTER MARGINS: 1" (left and right)
TYPEWRITER MARGINS: 15–70 (Pica)
                       25–80 (Elite)
SPACING: Single

1. **Review:** Type each line twice. Double space after each 2-line group.

Alphabet:	very buzz stew code flax ruse high main joke quips
1 2 3 6 7:	What is the sum of 12 and 16 and 37 and 73 and 62?
F:	fib fog fit; fox fop fur; fat few fun; fig fed fix
G:	get gob gut; gal gap gum; gig gag gun; gas gin god
Speedup:	The old man does good work and is fit for the job.

Use the correct finger for each number.

```
             1     2     3     4     5     6     7     8     9     10
```

2. **New-Key Practice: 5** *Use F-Finger.*
   Practice the reach from **F** to **5** and back home to **F**. Keep the **A**-finger at home. When you can reach **5** without looking at your fingers, type each line twice:

```
5 5 5 f5f f5f f5f 5 flags 5 flaps 5 fires 55 files
5 figs 5 fish 5 flew 5 fads 5 fix 5 fled 55 frames
Of the 25 students, 16 typed at 37 words a minute.
On June 1, there were 35 big ships in Fleet No. 5.
The correct answer to problem 52 is 5 3/5 exactly.
```

No. is the abbreviation for number. Space once after an abbreviation.

3. **New-Key Practice: 9** *Use L-Finger.*
   Practice the reach from **L** to **9** and back home to **L**. Try to keep the **J**-finger at home. When you can reach **9** without looking at your fingers, type each line twice:

```
9 9 9 191 191 191 9 lamps 9 loads 9 lambs 9 ladies
9 lids 9 legs 9 laws 9 lots 9 laps 9 lads 9 lights
Only 16 of the 59 typists made final grades of 95.
What is the sum of 19 and 25 and 36 and 73 and 95?
At 9:15 a.m., May 9, I flew to Paris on Flight 59.
```

No space after period between small initials.

LESSON 33
MASTERY DRILLS
AND TIMED TESTS

To help you master the keyboard, list the keys on which you often make errors. Then practice the drill for each key until you can type it smoothly and accurately.

Alphabet Keys

A	aa	aAa	alarms	animal	appear	attain	awaken	aa aAa
B	bb	bBb	babble	bribes	bubble	barber	blurbs	bb bBb
C	cc	cCc	circus	circle	cracks	cactus	clutch	cc cCc
D	dd	dDd	dawdle	addled	delude	deride	divide	dd dDd
E	ee	eEe	evenly	events	evolve	energy	emerge	ee eEe
F	ff	fFf	fifths	fluffs	fluffy	offers	suffer	ff fFf
G	gg	gGg	groggy	gauges	goggle	gargle	giggle	gg gGg
H	hh	hHh	health	height	hyphen	hushed	higher	hh hHh
I	ii	iIi	idioms	idiots	inning	incite	invite	ii iIi
J	jj	jJj	jalopy	juggle	junior	jejune	jujube	jj jJj
K	kk	kKk	kicker	knacks	knocks	kulaks	kopeck	kk kKk
L	ll	lLl	lilies	lulled	loller	lolled	llamas	ll lLl
M	mm	mMm	mimics	maxims	maimed	mammal	mammon	mm mMm
N	nn	nNn	ninety	nonage	noncom	nation	Newton	nn nNn
O	oo	oOo	oppose	oozing	onions	oblong	odious	oo oOo
P	pp	pPp	pepsin	pepper	papers	poplin	poplar	pp pPp
Q	qq	qQq	quirks	quacks	quaint	qualms	quarry	qq qQq
R	rr	rRr	rumors	rivers	repair	rarely	return	rr rRr
S	ss	sSs	shirts	sleeps	shreds	sister	series	ss sSs
T	tt	tTt	tattle	taunts	taught	tattoo	tatter	tt tTt
U	uu	uUu	usurer	usurps	future	upturn	Ursula	uu uUu
V	vv	vVv	valves	velvet	vivify	vervet	devolve	vv vVv
W	ww	wWw	winnow	widows	window	willow	wallow	ww wWw
X	xx	xXx	exerts	taxing	X-rays	Xerxes	boxing	xx xXx
Y	yy	yYy	yeasty	yellow	yearly	yonder	yachts	yy yYy
Z	zz	zZz	sizzle	guzzle	zigzag	buzzer	pizzas	zz zZz

4. **Paragraph Practice**: Double Spacing.
   Try for 2 PERFECT copies of this note:

WORDS

All the
alphabet
keys plus
all the
numbers
you know

Dear Zoel: 2

    Up to now, I sold 9 tickets for the August 25   12

game. Val Fox and Joe Quin sold 17; Pat, 16; Ben,   22

13; and Cy, 12. This makes a total of 67 tickets.   32

Tell coach Yardley that we are ahead of our quota.   42

    1   2   3   4   5   6   7   8   9   10

5. **Test Your Skill:** Take Three 2-Minute Timings.
   Goal: 18 words a minute within 4 errors.
             Record your best speed within 4 errors.

WORDS

    When a student gets that first job upon grad-   10

uation, he or she finds that the boss is much more   20

exact in a host of matters than were those patient   30

and kind teachers all liked so much at the school.   40

    1   2   3   4   5   6   7   8   9   10

```
;; if we want the stream to come from standard input, see
;; page 139

(define transition->current-state car)
(define transition->input cadr)
(define transition->next-state caddr)
(define transition->output cadddr)


;; ----------------------------------------------------------------
;; Now we cook the raw items

(define-record lexical-item (class data))


;;
;; ----------------------------------------------------------------
;; ----------------------------------------------------------------
;; Here are all the things that get passed on to the parser:
;;   integer-literal and variable and things in the next two lines:
(define *keywords* '(let in if then else proc begin end letrec define))
(define *tokens* '(assign-sym equal-sign lparen rparen semi))
;; ----------------------------------------------------------------
;; ----------------------------------------------------------------


(define cook-raw-item
  (lambda (item-class item-chars)
    (case item-class
      ((comment whitespace) #f)
      ((identifier)
       (let ((sym (string->symbol (apply string item-chars))))
         (if (memq sym *keywords*)
             (make-lexical-item sym '<ignored>)
             (make-lexical-item 'variable sym))))
      ((integer-literal)
       (make-lexical-item 'integer-literal (digit-list->number item-chars)))
      (else (if (memq item-class *tokens*)
                (make-lexical-item item-class '<ignored>)
                (error 'cook-raw-item "Unrecognized lexical class: ~s "
                   item-class))))))

(define digit-list->number
  (let ((code-for-zero (char->integer #\0)))
    (lambda (digit-list)
      (letrec
          ((loop (lambda (accumulator digit-list)
                   (if (null? digit-list)
                       accumulator
                       (loop (+ (* 10 accumulator)
                                (- (char->integer (car digit-list))
                                   code-for-zero))
                             (cdr digit-list))))))
        (loop 0 digit-list)))))
```

LESSON 18
NEW KEYS
4 8 0

1. **Review:** Type each line twice. Double space after each 2-line group.

Alphabet:	abc cde efg ghi ijk klm mno opq qrs stu uvwx xyzab
1 2 3 5 6 7 9:	Order 35 pads, 169 erasers, 236 pens, 327 pencils.
H:	hoe hop hum; hit had hut; him her hex; hew hen hog
I:	ill ice inn; ilk ire icy; ink imp Ida; Ina Ivy Ike
Speedup:	The old man who does good work will get a day off.

Try to start each line without a pause.

    1   2   3   4   5   6   7   8   9   10

2. **New-Key Practice: 4** *Use F-Finger.*
Practice the reach from **F** to **4** and back home to **F**. Keep the **A**-finger at home. When you can reach **4** without looking at your fingers, type each line twice:

```
4 4 4 f4f f4f f4f 4 flaps 4 flags 4 fires 4 firms;
4 figs 4 furs 4 fish 4 files 4 facts 4 farms 144.4
About 44 boys took the 14-mile hike June 14, 1944.
Add these figures:  4 and 14 and 49 and 64 and 74.
The 14 boys caught the 4:15 p.m. train on Track 4.
```

3. **New-Key Practice: 8** *Use K-Finger.*
Practice the reach from **K** to **8** and back home to **K**. Keep **;**-finger in home position. When you can reach **8** without looking at your fingers, type each line twice:

```
8 8 8 k8k k8k k8k 8 knots 8 knobs 8 kites 8 kinds;
8 keys 8 kings 8 kits 8 kids 8 kegs 8 killed 48.14
What is the sum of 8 and 48 and 84 and 88 and 418?
The 84 men worked a total of 484 hours on July 18.
Vince will call tomorrow at 8:15 A.M. or 4:15 P.M.
```

Space once after period following capital initials.

LISP

```
;; An example of the use of a procedure in this style
(next-raw-item automaton1 '(#\B #\b #\space #\$)
    (lambda (item-class item-chars unused-char-stream)
      (write (list item-class item-chars unused-char-stream))
      (newline)
      (next-raw-item automaton1 unused-char-stream list)))


;;-------------------------------------------------------
;;  STREAMS:
;; Naive helper functions for (very) finite streams
;; that can be represented as lists
(define first car)
(define rest cdr)
(define make-stream
  (lambda (value thunk)
    (cons value (thunk))))
(define the-empty-stream
  (lambda ()
    '()))
(define empty-stream? null?)

;; and the slightly higher level functions that use them to do
;; operations on streams
(define stream-for-each
  (lambda (proc stream)
    (letrec ((loop (lambda (stream)
                     (if (not (empty-stream? stream))
                         (begin
                           (proc (first stream))
                           (loop (rest stream)))))))
      (loop stream))))

(define display-stream
  (lambda (stream)
    (stream-for-each display stream)
    (newline)))

(define string->stream
  (lambda (string)
    (let ((len (string-length string)))
      (letrec ((loop (lambda (n)
                       (if (= n len)
                           (the-empty-stream)
                           (make-stream)
                             (string-ref string n)
                             (lambda ()
                               (loop (+ n 1)))))))
        (loop 0)))))
```

4. **New-Key Practice: 0** *Use ;-Finger.*
   Practice the reach from **;** to **0** and back home to **;**. Keep the **J**-finger at home. Keep elbow close to body. When you can reach **0** without looking at your fingers, type each line twice.

   ```
   0 0 0 ;0; ;0; ;0; 10 pins 10 pals 10 pads 10 packs
   10 pets 10 pews 10 pegs 10 plums 10 plays 10 plans
   The teams will practice at 10:30 a.m. or 2:30 p.m.
   There were 150 to 170 men at the March 10 meeting.
   Buzzy is 10 years 10 months and 10 days old today.
   ```

5. **Paragraph Practice:** Double Spacing.
   Try for 2 PERFECT copies of this note:

   WORDS

The whole alphabet and all the numbers.

```
Dear Walt:                                              2

     I have arranged to have the Annual Banquet of     12

The Commercial Club meet at the Duke Hotel on June     22

9 at 8:00 p.m. in Room 1364.  I expect at least 25     32

of our members to attend.  Please manage to return     42

all unsold tickets to Mr. Zims by Tuesday, June 7.     52
     1     2     3     4     5     6     7     8     9     10
```

6. **Test Your Skill:** Take Three 2-Minute Timings.
   Goal: 18 words a minute within 4 errors.
   Record your best speed within 4 errors.

   WORDS

Use double spacing.

```
     You will not learn much that counts if you do     10
not have the urge to learn.  This is a thought you     20
may well ponder.  You should strive to equip your-     30
self with the skills to excel in the job you have.     40
     1     2     3     4     5     6     7     8     9     10
```

Lesson 18: 4 8 0   43

```
/**********************************************************************/
/*****    pos = length of input file in bytes.                  *****/
/*****    outbytes = length of output file in bytes             *****/
/*****    shift = amount to shift buffer into buffer1 to compress bits *****/
/*****    overflow = the case where left bits + 16 mod 11 > 1   *****/
/*****    prev = holds previous 16 bits to retrieve the bits left over *****/
/*****    overleft = the new left when overflow = 16+leftbits % 11 *****/
/*****    buffer = holds the current codeword                   *****/
/*****    buffer1 = holds data to compress bits into output     *****/
/*****    nextbit = singles out bits for shift register (low-end first)*****/
/*****    r1,r2,r3,r4 = shift register stages                   *****/
/**********************************************************************/

int iflag=0, oflag=0;
int f1,f2;
int cc;
char d;
long loopval,pos,outbytes;
unsigned short count=0,shift,overflow = 0;
```

LESSON 19
HORIZONTAL CENTERING

COMPUTER MARGINS: 1" (left and right)
TYPEWRITER MARGINS: 15–70 (Pica)
                        25–80 (Elite)
SPACING: Single

1. **New-Key Practice: Backspace** *Use ;-Finger.*
   Practice the reach from **;** to backspace and back to home row.   Sit erect;
   A. Type each line as it appears.   feet flat on
   B. Hit the backspace and fill in the missing "a" in each word.   floor.

   ```
   J:  j m, j w, j r, j b, j il, j de, j unt.
   K:  k t, ke , ko , k y, ky k, k le, ko l .
   ```

2. **Horizontal Centering:** Horizontal centering means typing a word or line so that half of it is on each side of the center of the paper.
   A. Standard typing paper is 8½ inches wide.
   B. Pica type (large) measures 10 characters per inch.
      So: 8½ inches × 10 = 85 Pica characters across the paper.
   C. Elite type (small) measures 12 characters per inch.
      So: 8½ inches × 12 = 102 Elite characters across the paper.
   D. The center of 8½-inch paper is 42 (Pica); 50 (Elite).

To center horizontally:

A. Clear all the tab settings on the typewriter. Set a tab stop at the center of the paper.
B. Insert the paper with its left edge at "0" on the paper-guide scale.
C. Tabulate to the center of the paper—hold down the tab key till the carriage stops.
D. Backspace once for every 2 letters, numbers, punctuation marks, or spaces in the line.
   Say the strokes in pairs, depressing the backspacer once as you say each pair. Do not backspace for an odd letter at the end.
E. Begin typing when you finish backspacing.

NOTE: If you are using a computer, check your user manual for automatic horizontal centering instructions for your software.

C

```
/tmp/encoder.c        Wed Dec 27 15:21:10 19XX

#include <stdio.h>
#include <strings.h>
#include <sys/file.h>
#include <math.h>
/**********************************************************************/
/*****                  BCH Encoder based on GF(2 ^ n-k)         ****/
/*****                                                           ****/
/*****   This encoder is for a (15,11) BCH code. Here are some specs ****/
/*****   on this particular code:                                ****/
/*****                                                           ****/
/*****               Input Block Length : 11 bits               ****/
/*****               Codeword Length    : 15 bits               ****/
/*****               Bit Expansion      : approx. 27%           ****/
/*****               # Parity checks    : 15 - 11 = 4           ****/
/*****               Error correction   : 1                     ****/
/*****                                                           ****/
/*****   The low order 11 bits of every codeword is equal to the ****/
/*****   input block. The 4 parity check digits are determined  ****/
/*****   using the following circuit:                           ****/
/*****                                                           ****/
/*****    ----> R1 ----> + ------> R2 -------> R3 --------> R4 --->  ****/
/*****    ^              ^                                  |    ****/
/*****    |              |                                  |    ****/
/*****    |              |                                  |    ****/
/*****    + ---------------------------------------------<-  ****/
/*****    |                                                      ****/
/*****  u(x)                                                     ****/
/*****                                                           ****/
/*****   The input block u(x) is fed into the shift register low ****/
/*****   order first. When all of the digits have been fed into ****/
/*****   the circuit, the contents of the registers, R1-R4, are ****/
/*****   your parity check digits.                              ****/
/*****                                                           ****/
/*****                 A More Generalized Explanation           ****/
/*****                 ------------------------------           ****/
/*****   An encoding circuit for an (n,k) BCH code has n-k stages. ****/
/*****   Based on Galois field theory, every BCH code has what is ****/
/*****   called a primitive polynomial, which by theory has degree ****/
/*****   less than or equal to n-k. Based on this polynomial, the ****/
/*****   circuit can be derived. For further explanation, refer to ****/
/*****   pp. 117-118 of Berlekamp's "The Development of Coding  ****/
/*****   Theory."                                               ****/
/**********************************************************************/
```

Lesson 32: Computer Languages

EXAMPLES:

A. *To center the word* TYPING:
   1.. Tabulate to the center of the paper.
   2. Backspace once for every 2 letters:

   TY PI NG

   3. Type the word.

Using the backspace key: Use a light, quick stroke; release quickly to avoid a double backspace.

B. *To center the word* SHORTHAND:
   1. Tabulate to the center of the paper.
   2. Backspace once for every 2 letters:

   SH OR TH AN (Do not backspace for D)

   3. Type the word.

C. *To center the words* BUSINESS TRAINING:
   1. Tabulate to the center of the paper.
   2. Backspace once for every 2 letters and spaces:

   BU SI NE SS space T RA IN IN
   (Do not backspace for G)

   3. Type the words.
      Check: The words in Examples A, B, and C, when centered, should appear like this:

   TYPING
   SHORTHAND
   BUSINESS TRAINING

3. **Centering Practice:** A. Center each line in each group.
                          B. Double space after each group.

Accuracy	Efficiency
Touch Typing	The Merit System
Horizontal Centering	Success in Business
Stenography	The Empire State Building
Transcription	34 Street and Fifth Avenue
Office Manager	New York, NY ZIP

```
               02   00EF   97         .byte    2
               A6   00F0   98         .byte    ^XA6
20 20 77 76 69 64   00F1   99         .ascii   /divw  /
               02   00F7   100        .byte    2
               C6   00F8   101        .byte    ^XC6
20 20 6C 76 69 64   00F9   102        .ascii   /divl  /
               02   00FF   103        .byte    2
               9F   0100   104        .byte    ^X9F
62 61 68 73 75 70   0101   105        .ascii   /pushab/
               01   0107   106        .byte    1
               3F   0108   107        .byte    ^X3F
77 61 68 73 75 70   0109   108        .ascii   /pushaw/
               01   010F   109        .byte    1
               DF   0110   110        .byte    ^XDF
6C 61 68 73 75 70   0111   111        .ascii   /pushal/
               01   0117   112        .byte    1
               00   0118   113        .byte    ^X00
20 20 74 6C 61 68   0119   114        .ascii   /halt  /
```

4. **Paragraph Practice:** Double Spacing.
   A. Type each paragraph twice—slowly, smoothly.
   B. Practice each word that has an error.
   C. Try for a PERFECT copy of each paragraph.

WORDS

All the
number
keys.

Christopher Sholes, born on February 14, 1819,   10

made the first practical typewriter. He got a pat-   20

ent for his machine in 1868. Touch typing, though,   30

was first introduced in 1878 by Frank E. McGurrin.   40

   1   2   3   4   5   6   7   8   9   10

Oliver Wendell Holmes was born March 8, 1841.   10

He graduated from Harvard in 1861 and from Harvard   20

Law School in 1866. He was appointed a Justice of   30

the Supreme Court in 1902. He died March 6, 1935.   40

   1   2   3   4   5   6   7   8   9   10

5. **Test Your Skill:** Take Three 2-Minute Timings.
   Goal: 18 words a minute within 4 errors.
           Record your best speed within 4 errors.

WORDS

Use
double
spacing.

Good skill, of course, will help you get that   10
job. Yet it is not enough to make you hold it and   20
get ahead in it. You must also learn to work well   30
with the others in a helpful and energetic spirit.   40

   1   2   3   4   5   6   7   8   9   10

```
20 20 77 63 69 62    0069    48              .ascii    /bicw  /
             02      006F    49              .byte     2
             CA      0070    50              .byte     ^XCA
20 20 6C 63 69 62    0071    51              .ascii    /bicl  /
             02      0077    52              .byte     2
             12      0078    53              .byte     ^X12
20 20 71 65 6E 62    0079    54              .ascii    /bneq  /
             01      007F    55              .byte     1
             97      0080    56              .byte     ^X97
20 20 62 63 65 64    0081    57              .ascii    /decb  /
             01      0087    58              .byte     1
             B7      0088    59              .byte     ^XB7
20 20 77 63 65 64    0089    60              .ascii    /decw  /
             01      008F    61              .byte     1
             D7      0090    62              .byte     ^XD7
20 20 6C 63 65 64    0091    63              .ascii    /decl  /
             01      0097    64              .byte     1
             85      0098    65              .byte     ^X85
20 20 62 6C 75 6D    0099    66              .ascii    /mulb  /
             03      009F    67              .byte     3
             A5      00A0    68              .byte     ^XA5
20 20 77 6C 75 6D    00A1    69              .ascii    /mulw  /
             03      00A7    70              .byte     3
             C5      00A8    71              .byte     ^XC5
20 20 6C 6C 75 6D    00A9    72              .ascii    /mull  /
             03      00AF    73              .byte     3
             95      00B0    74              .byte     ^X95
20 20 62 74 73 74    00B1    75              .ascii    /tstb  /
             01      00B7    76              .byte     1
             B5      00B8    77              .byte     ^XB5
20 20 77 74 73 74    00B9    78              .ascii    /tstw  /
             01      00BF    79              .byte     1
             D5      00C0    80              .byte     ^XD5
20 20 6C 74 73 74    00C1    81              .ascii    /tstl  /
             01      00C7    82              .byte     1
             8B      00C8    83              .byte     ^X8B
20 20 62 63 69 62    00C9    84              .ascii    /bicb  /
             03      00CF    85              .byte     3
             AB      00D0    86              .byte     ^XAB
20 20 77 63 69 62    00D1    87              .ascii    /bicw  /
             03      00D7    88              .byte     3
             CB      00D8    89              .byte     ^XCB
20 20 6C 63 69 62    00D9    90              .ascii    /bicl  /
             03      00DF    91              .byte     3
             12      00E0    92              .byte     ^X12
20 75 71 65 6E 62    00E1    93              .ascii    /bnequ /
             01      00E7    94              .byte     1
             86      00E8    95              .byte     ^X86
20 20 62 76 69 64    00E9    96              .ascii    /divb  /
```

LESSON 20
VERTICAL CENTERING

1. **Review:** Type each line twice. Double space after each 2-line group.

Alphabet: `The broken trapeze was quickly fixed by Jim Gavor.`   Aim for a
   ?: `;?; ;?; ;?; ?; who? why? when? whom? where? which?`   quick return
   L: `lap lot leg; lab lax law; lid lug lay; low let lip`   to margin.
   M: `may mid mug; mad mat man; mop mob met; mud mum mew`
Speedup: `If the old man is sick, he will get four days off.`

      1   2   3   4   5   6   7   8   9   10

2. **Vertical Centering:** Vertical centering means typing material so that it appears with equal top and bottom margins.
   A. Standard typing paper is 11 inches long.
   B. Typewriters space 6 lines to the inch.
   > So: A full sheet has 11 × 6 = 66 lines.
   > A half sheet has 5½ × 6 = 33 lines.

To center vertically:

(1) Count the typed and blank lines in the copy.
(2) Subtract the total lines from the number of lines available on your paper—66 or 33.
(3) Divide the remainder by 2. The answer is the line number on which to start typing. Drop any fraction.

EXAMPLE A: *To center 25 lines on a full sheet:*
    (1) Subtract 25 from 66. Answer: 41.
    (2) Divide 41 by 2. Answer: 20½. Drop the fraction.
    (3) Start typing on line 20 from top edge of the paper.

EXAMPLE B: *To center 12 lines on a half sheet:*
    (1) Subtract 12 from 33. Answer: 21.
    (2) Divide 21 by 2. Answer: 10½. Drop the fraction.
    (3) Start typing on line 10 from top edge of the paper.

NOTE: If you are using a computer, check your user manual for the software you are using for automatic page preview instructions.

ASSEMBLY

```
                    0000    1 ;***************************************************
                    0000    2 ;***    Programming assignment #4      Scott Sampson ***
                    0000    3 ;***    Comp. Organization & Prog. I     023-64-0550  ***
                    0000    4 ;***    Professor Bugrara              Feb 23, 19XX  ***
                    0000    5 ;***************************************************
                    0000    6 ;
                    0000    7 Table: ;Table Of Opcodes & # of Oper.
                 80 0000    8              .byte      ^X80
20 32 62 64 64 61 0001    9              .ascii     /addb2 /
                 02 0007   10              .byte      2
                 A0 0008   11              .byte      ^XA0
20 32 77 64 64 61 0009   12              .ascii     /addw2 /
                 02 000F   13              .byte      2
                 C0 0010   14              .byte      ^XC0
20 32 6C 64 64 61 0011   15              .ascii     /addl2 /
                 02 0017   16              .byte      2
                 81 0018   17              .byte      ^X81
20 33 62 64 64 61 0019   18              .ascii     /addb3 /
                 03 001F   19              .byte      3
                 A1 0020   20              .byte      ^XA1
20 33 77 64 64 61 0021   21              .ascii     /addw3 /
                 03 0027   22              .byte      3
                 C1 0028   23              .byte      ^XC1
20 33 6C 64 64 61 0029   24              .ascii     /addl3 /
                 03 002F   25              .byte      3
                 90 0030   26              .byte      ^X90
20 20 62 76 6F 6D 0031   27              .ascii     /movb  /
                 02 0037   28              .byte      2
                 B0 0038   29              .byte      ^XB0
20 20 77 76 6F 6D 0039   30              .ascii     /movw  /
                 02 003F   31              .byte      2
                 D0 0040   32              .byte      ^XD0
20 20 6C 76 6F 6D 0041   33              .ascii     /movl  /
                 02 0047   34              .byte      2
                 9E 0048   35              .byte      ^X9E
20 62 61 76 6F 6D 0049   36              .ascii     /movab /
                 02 004F   37              .byte      2
                 3E 0050   38              .byte      ^X3E
20 77 61 76 6F 6D 0051   39              .ascii     /movaw /
                 02 0057   40              .byte      2
                 DE 0058   41              .byte      ^XDE
20 6C 61 76 6F 6D 0059   42              .ascii     /moval /
                 02 005F   43              .byte      2
                 8A 0060   44              .byte      ^X8A
20 20 62 63 69 62 0061   45              .ascii     /bicb  /
                 02 0067   46              .byte      2
                 AA 0068   47              .byte      ^XAA
```

BUSINESS COURSES
Evening Classes

Job 1 (Tryout)
Center on a
full sheet.

Write or Phone
For
Free Bulletin

BERNARD M. BARUCH COLLEGE
17 Lexington Avenue
New York, NY 10010

Phone 673–7700
7:00 to 9:30 p.m.

To leave
one blank
line in
single-
spaced
typing, use
the return
lever or key
twice.

Let us plan and center Job 1:

1. A. Clear the machine.
    B. Set a tab stop at the center of the paper.
    C. Set line-space regulator for single spacing.

2. A. Count the typed lines 10
    B. Count the blank lines ....<u>3</u>
       Total lines in the advertisement 13

3. A. Jot down the total lines in a full sheet 66
    B. Subtract the total lines in the advertisement ....<u>13</u>
       Total lines left over for top and bottom margins 53

4. A. Divide total lines left over by 2: 53 ÷ 2 = 26½ or 26.
    B. Space down 26 lines from top edge of the paper.

5. A. Tabulate to the center of the paper.
    B. Backspace once for every 2 strokes in the first line.
    C. Type the line.
       Repeat these 3 steps till you have centered all the lines.

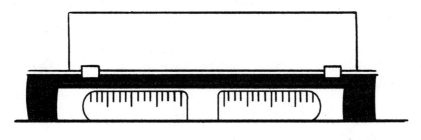

Aligning scale.

The aligning scale may be on each side of the point where the type bar or ball strikes the paper.
Make sure that top edge of the paper is even with top of aligning scale.

```
80        C****************************************************************
81        C***              IF NOT VALID CALENDAR DATE RE-KEY          ***
82        C****************************************************************
83        C     99                  GOTO DATET
84        C                         SETON                         97
85        C          DATEOK         TAG
86        C                         EXSR DATECM
87        C*
88        C          RECTPE         COMP 'EB'                           92
89        C          D2             COMP D5                        13
90        C     92N13 PBALFD        ADD  AMOUNT    PBALFD 82
91        C     N92N13 CBALFD       ADD  AMOUNT    CBALFD 82
92        C     13    OPENAM        ADD  AMOUNT    OPENAM 82
93        C      N13  SUBTOT        ADD  AMOUNT    SUBTOT 82
94        C          END            TAG
95        C     U1                  SETON                         LR
96        CL1        OPENAM         ADD  SUBTOT    TOTREC 82
97        C*
98        C****************************************************************
99        C***    THIS SUBROUTINE PUTS THE DATE IN THE FORM:          ***
100       C***                  YY/MM/DD                              ***
101       C****************************************************************
102       CSR        DATECM         BEGSR
103       CSR                       MOVELYR        D1     40
104       CSR                       MOVE MO        D1
105       CSR                       MOVELD1        D2     60
106       CSR                       MOVE DY        D2              FILE DATE
107       CSR                       MOVELDATE      D3     40
108       CSR                       MOVE DATE      D4     20
109       CSR                       MOVELD4        D5     60
110       CSR                       MOVE D3        D5              ENTRD DATE
111       CSR                       ENDSR
112       CSR        DATECH         BEGSR
113       C****************************************************************
114       C***      SUBROUTINE FOR DETERMINING VALID CALENDAR DATES   ***
115       C***                                                        ***
116       C***          SUB-ROUTINE WILL VALIDATE DATE               ***
117       C***            99    INVALID DATE ERROR.                  ***
118       C***        INDICATORS USE  01, 02, 21, 29, 99.            ***
119       C***                                                        ***
120       C****************************************************************
```

3. **Practice:** Center Jobs 2, 3, and 4 vertically and horizontally.

Job 2
Center on a
full sheet.
(66 lines)

TYPISTS

We Need You

EXCELLENT STARTING SALARY

Paid Vacations
Paid Holidays
Paid Health Insurance
Paid Sick Leave

BARTON CAREER AGENCY
137 West 42 Street
New York, NY 10014

Call Miss Ostend
212-608-9501

NOTE: To center vertically on a half sheet, subtract total lines from 33.

Job 3
Center on a
half sheet.

A HIGH SCHOOL DIPLOMA
Will Help You
To Get
A Better Job
STAY IN SCHOOL

Job 4
Center on a
half sheet.

SATURDAY
LUNCHEON

Chicken Gumbo Soup

Chopped Steak Sandwich
on Toast

Ice Cream or Fruit Cup

Milk or Coffee

```
30           F*    1  07/30/XX   SAS    PAR7409                              *
31           F*       MODIFICATIONS MADE TO PROCESS ALL BRANCHES
32           F*       AT ONE TIME...
33           F*                                                              *
34           F*-----------------------------------------------------------*
35           FEMPRECV IP  F  64   64              DISC
36           FSYSCNTRLUC  F 256  256R06AI     1 DISC
37           FKEY      D  F  40   40
38           FRECCUR   O  F  64   64              DISC
39           FRECFUT   O  F  64   64              DISC
40           FREPORT   O  F 132  132       OF    LP
41           E                      MESS2    1   1 22
42      0020 E                      MESS     1   3 60
43           IEMPRECV NS  03
44           I                                     1   2 RECTPE
45           I                                     3  60BRANCHL1
46           I                                 P  59  622AMOUNT
47           I                                    13 140MO
48           I                                    15 160DY
49           I                                    17 180YR
50           I                                     1  64 DATA
51           ISYSCNTRLNS  04    5 CS    6 CC
52           I                                     7  26 BRNAME
53           I           NS  05    5 CA    6 CR
54           I                                     7 120WEDATE
55           C*******************************************************
56           C                      SETOF                    13
57           C   NL1                GOTO DATET
58           C*
59           C*******************************************************
60           C***             KEY BRANCH AND CHAIN TO SYSCNTRL     ***
61           C***                 - REKEY IF NOT FOUND -           ***
62           C*******************************************************
63           C                      MOVELBRANCH   SYSCH    6
64           C                      MOVE 'SC'     SYSCH
65           C         SYSCH        CHAINSYSCNTRL            23
66           C   23                 Z-ADD1        X        10
67           C   23                 GOTO ERR
68           C                      MOVE 'AR'     SYSCH
69           C         SYSCH        CHAINSYSCNTRL            24
70           C   24                 Z-ADD2        X        10
71           C   24                 GOTO ERR
72           C                      GOTO DATET
73           C         ERR          TAG
74           C                      SETON                    U1
75           C                      GOTO END
76           C         DATET        TAG
77           C   97                 GOTO DATEOK
78           C         MESS2,1      DSPLYKEY      DATE     60
79           C                      EXSR DATECH
```

4. **Paragraph Practice:** Double Spacing.
   Try for a PERFECT copy of each paragraph:

All the
number
keys.

       Franklin D. Roosevelt, born January 30, 1882,   10

became President March 4, 1933. He was re-elected   20

in 1936, 1940, 1944. On August 14, 1941, he aided   30

in drafting the structure of the Atlantic Charter.   40

    1   2   3   4   5   6   7   8   9   10

       After the attack on Pearl Harbor, December 7,   10

1941, he began to plan for victory in World War 2.   20

In Axis aggression he saw a threat to our liberty.   30

He died at Warm Springs, Georgia, April 12, 1945.   40

    1   2   3   4   5   6   7   8   9   10

5. **Test Your Skill:** Take Three 2-Minute Timings.
   Goal: 18 words a minute within 4 errors.
         Record your best speed within 4 errors.

All the
alphabet
keys.

       No type of job you have is worthwhile if you   10

do the work lazily till quitting time. If you are   20

eager to make good in business or any other field,   30

get into the type of work in which you can put in   40

full time and exert your best efforts for success.   50

    1   2   3   4   5   6   7   8   9   10

```
7.3
7.4
7.5    DATA DIVISION.
7.6    FILE SECTION.
7.7
7.8    ************************************************************
7.9    FD   SYSTEM-CONTROL-FILE
8           RECORD CONTAINS 256 CHARACTERS
8.1         DATA RECORD IS RA-SYS-CONTROL-RECORD.
8.2
8.3    COPY RASYSCNT.
9.1    ************************************************************
9.2    FD   PROCESS-DATE-FILE
```

RPG II

```
1            $CONTROL QUOTE=',USLINIT
2            H          JF    1                    B      X1 N        0 0
3            F* MOD # 1 - AR0005 - S.SAMPSON - 07/30/XX -  PAR7409
4            F* * * * * * * * * * NEW CODE LOG * * * * * * * * * * * *
5            F*     WRITTEN BY:  S.DUPUY                             *
6            F*   DATE WRITTEN:  09/21/XX                            *
7            F*   PROGRAM NAME:  AR0005                              *
8            F*    SERVICE REQ:                                      *
9            F*        PURPOSE:                                      *
10           F* SELECT CURRENT EMPLOYEE RECEIVABLES FOR EMPLOYEE STATEMENTS
11           F* SELECT ALL CURRENT EMPLOYEE TRANSACTIONS FROM THE EMPRECV FILE
12           F* FOR ONE OUTPUT FILE (RECCUR) AND ALL FUTURE EMPLOYEE TRANSACTIONS
13           F* FOR THE OUTPUT FILE (RECFUT) - THE DATE IS KEYED IN WITH THE
14           F* BRANCH AND THE BRANCH IS SAVED IN A WORKFILE TO BE PASSED TO THE
15           F* NEXT PROGRAM (AR0006) - IT ALSO POINTS A SUMMARY REPORT OF THE
16           F* TOTAL RECEIVABLES AND ITEMS SELECTED FOR DEDUCTION.  IT WILL ALSO
17           F* UPDATE THE CONTROL DATE FOR EMPLOYEE RECEIVABLES IN THE SYSTEM
18           F* CONTROL FILE
19           F*                                                      *
20           F*                                                      *
21           F* PROGRAM LOGIC:                                       *
22           F*                                                      *
23           F*                                                      *
24           F*                                                      *
25           F* * * * * * * * * * * * * * * * * * * * * * * * * * * * *
26           F* * * * * * * PROGRAM MODIFICATION LOG * * * * * * * * *
27           F* MOD. MOD.  PROG   S/R              SUMMARY           *
28           F*  #   DATE  INIT    #          OF ACTUAL MODIFICATION *
29           F*------------------------------------------------------*
```

LESSON 21
NEW KEYS
¢ (Cents) ½ (One-Half)

COMPUTER MARGINS: 1" (left and right)
TYPEWRITER MARGINS: 15–70 (Pica)
25–80 (Elite)
SPACING: Single

1. **Review:** Type each line twice. Double space after each 2-line group.

Alphabet: quit wavy exit cubs hems park jolt done zero flags

All Numbers: Type these numbers: 1910, 1928, 1939, 1947, 1956.

N: nut nag not; nip nap nub; now nod new; net nab nib

O: old out ode; one owe oak; owl off oil; ohm oaf ore

Speedup: All men on this job who do good work get good pay.

        1   2   3   4   5   6   7   8   9   10

Type only with your fingers; wrists and elbows still.

2. **New-Key Practice:** ¢
The ¢ is on the **6**-key. Use **J**-finger. (1) Depress left shift key; (2) Reach for the **6**-key; (3) Move fingers back home. Practice these steps until you can do them smoothly without looking at your fingers. Then type this drill twice:

No space between a number and the sign ¢.

¢ ¢ ¢ j¢j j¢j j¢j The items are 6¢, 16¢, 26¢, 36¢.

```
¢
6
```

Type each line twice.

Ship 3 doz. at 20¢; 6 at 26¢; 8 at 30¢; 38 at 46¢.
Our items are marked 10¢, 36¢, 47¢, 59¢, 64¢, 93¢.
Jackie bought 5 oranges at 8¢; 6 at 9¢; 12 at 10¢.
Get 1 pair at 30¢; 3 pairs at 56¢; 8 pairs at 70¢.
Buy 15 stamps at 6¢; 7 at 8¢; 9 at 10¢; 14 at 12¢.

All the number keys.

3. **New-Key Practice:** ½ *Use ;-Finger.*
Practice the reach from **;** to ½ and back home to **;**. Keep the **J**-finger in home position. When you can reach the ½ without looking at your fingers, type each line twice:

No space between a number and the sign ½.

½ ½ ;½; ;½; ;½; ½ hour; ½ week; ½ month; ½ year;
;½; ;½; ;½; The sum of 10½ and 15½ and 20½ is 46½.
Yes, 3 is ½ of 6; 4½ is ½ of 9 and 7½ is ½ of 15.
The swimming pool is 25½ feet long, 14½ feet wide.
I walked 2½ miles in a half hour; 4½, in one hour.

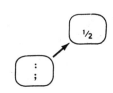

NOTE: The symbols are slightly different on a typewriter from those on a computer. If you are using a computer, check your manual for the software you are using for how to access special symbols. For example, ¢, ½, @, ®, ™, and many more.

COBOL

```
1       $CONTROL USLINIT,MAP,VERBS
1.1     IDENTIFICATION DIVISION.
1.2     PROGRAM-ID.    RAD095C.
1.3     AUTHOR.        S. SAMPSON.
1.4     INSTALLATION.  GENERAL-CINEMA-BEVERAGES.
1.5     DATE-WRITTEN.  10/30/87.
1.6     DATE-COMPILED. 11/02/87.
1.7
1.8     * [MOD 0 - RAD095C - S. SAMPSON    - 11/02/XX - SR# PRS7504]
1.9     * * * * * * * * * * * * * NEW CODE LOG  * * * * * * * * * * *
2       *  WRITTEN BY : S. SAMPSON                                  *
2.1     *  DATE WRITTEN: 02 NOVEMBER 19XX                           *
2.2     *  PROGRAM NAME: RAD095C                                    *
2.3     *  SERVICE REQ : PRS7504                                    *
2.4     *   PURPOSE:  TO VERIFY THE PROCESSING DATE ENTERED BY      *
2.5     *               THE USER DURING ROUTE SETTLEMENT BY COMPARING *
2.51    *               IT TO THE DATE IN THE RASYSCNT FILE....     *
2.6     *   PROGRAM LOGIC:                                          *
4.4     *                                                           *
4.5     *   FILES USED:  RASTW04J, RASTW04S                         *
4.6     * * * * * * * * * * * * * * * * * * * * * * * * * * * * * * *
4.7     * * * * * * * * * PROGRAM MODIFICATION LOG * * * * * * * * * *
4.8     * MOD. MOD.  PROG   S/R              SUMMARY                *
4.9     * #   DATE   INIT    #          OF ACTUAL MODIFICATION      *
5       *----------------------------------------------------------*
5.1     *                                                          *
5.2     *----------------------------------------------------------*
5.3     ENVIRONMENT DIVISION.
5.4     CONFIGURATION SECTION.
5.5
5.6     SOURCE-COMPUTER.   HP-3000.
5.7     OBJECT-COMPUTER.   HP-3000.
5.8
5.9     INPUT-OUTPUT SECTION.
6       FILE-CONTROL.
6.1
6.2     SELECT SYSTEM-CONTROL-FILE
6.3         ASSIGN TO "RASYSCNT"
6.4         ORGANIZATION IS SEQUENTIAL
6.5         ACCESS IS SEQUENTIAL
6.6         FILE STATUS IS SYS-CNTRL-STAT.
6.7
6.8     SELECT PROCESS-DATE-FILE
6.9         ASSIGN TO "WORKFILE"
7           ORGANIZATION IS SEQUENTIAL
7.1         ACCESS IS SEQUENTIAL
7.2         FILE STATUS IS PROCESS-DATE-FILE-STAT.
```

4. **Paragraph Practice:** Double Spacing.
   Try for 2 PERFECT copies of this paragraph:

We have the following orders to fill: 58 for   10

size 2½ at 14¢; 20 for size 3½ at 26¢; 78 for size   20

4½ at 17¢; 83 for size 5½ at 19¢; 35 for size 6 at   30

23¢; 50 for size 6½ at 27¢; 9 for size 10½ at 40¢.   40

  1   2   3   4   5   6   7   8   9   10

5. **Test Your Skill:** Take Three 3-Minute Timings.

Follow these steps in all your 3-minute timings.

A. Repeat if you finish before end of 3 minutes.
B. After each timing, jot down total words typed and total errors.
   Practice the words that have errors till they are easy for you.
C. Your 3-minute speed is words typed divided by 3.
D. Record on your Progress Chart (page 153) your best speed within 4 errors.
   Goal: 20 words a minute within 4 errors.

WORDS

The mature person bears the accidents of life   10

with grace and dignity, making the best of things.   20

Your mind is like your stomach; it is not how   30

much you put into it, but how much you can digest.   40

The value of an education lies in the ability   50

to make a living out of the know—how you acquired.   60

  1   2   3   4   5   6   7   8   9   10

Lesson 21: ¢ ½

BASIC

```
10 'RCHANGE
20 'CHRISTA BAYER   08/23/XX
30 'PROGRAM CHANGES A RECORD ON FILE
40 '************   DATA DICTIONARY
50 'L$...... LICENSE NUMBER ...INPUT
60 'BL$..... BUFFER LICENSE NUMBER
70 'N$...... NEW NAME ...INPUT
80 'BN$..... BUFFER NAME
1000 '*********   CONTROL MODULE
1010 CLEAR 2000
1020 GOSUB 2000
1030 PRINT"ENTER LICENSE NO. OR END"
1040 LINE INPUT L$
1050 IF L$="END" THEN CLOSE #1: END ELSE GOSUB 3000
1060 GOTO 1030
2000 '*********   INITIALIZATION
2005 CLS
2010 POKE 16916,2
2020 PRINT"CHANGES NAME ON RECORD OF DRIVERS LICENSE"
2025 PRINT
2030 OPEN "R",1,"CBRFILE"
2040 FIELD #1,1 AS B1$,15 AS BL$,20 AS BN$
2050 RETURN
3000 '**********   SEARCH
3010 LET R=1
3020 GET #1,R
3030 IF L$=BL$ THEN GOSUB 4000: RETURN
3040 LET R=R+1
3050 IF EOF(1) THEN GOSUB 5000: RETURN
3060 GOTO 3020
4000 '************  FOUND ROUTINE
4005 CLS
4010 PRINT"ENTER NEW NAME"
4020 LINE INPUT N$
4030 CLS
4040 PRINT"FORMER NAME:    ";BN$
4050 PRINT
4060 PRINT"NEW NAME:        ";N$
4070 PRINT
4080 PRINT"IS NEW NAME CORRECT"
4090 LINE INPUT Q$
4100 IF Q$="Y" THEN LSET BN$=N$:PUT #1, R ELSE 4005
4110 RETURN
5000 '***********  NOT FOUND ROUTINE
5010 CLS
5020 PRINT"LICENSE NUMBER NOT ON FILE"
5030 FOR X=1 TO 1000: NEXT X
5040 RETURN
```

LESSON 22
NEW KEYS
$ (Dollars) ' (Apostrophe)

1. **Review:** Type each line twice. Double space after each 2-line group.

Alphabet: abc cde efg ghi ijk klm mno opq qrs stu uvwx xyzab
½: ;½; ;½; ;½; The sum of 14½ and 25½ and 39½ is 79½.
¢: ¢ ¢ ¢ j¢j j¢j j¢j Toys are 66¢, 76¢, 86¢, and 96¢.
Speedup: That farm work is too hard for old men to do well.
  1 2 3 4 5 6 7 8 9 10

Good posture helps you to avoid errors.

2. **New-Key Practice: $** *Use F-Finger.*
The **$** is on the **4**-key. (1) Depress right shift key; (2) Reach for the **4**-key; (3) Move fingers back home. When you can do these 3 steps smoothly without looking at your fingers, type each line twice:

No space between the sign $ and a number.

$ $ $ f$f f$f f$f Give $40 or $41, not $45 or $46.
f$f f$f f$f Get the jar for $4; the jug for $4.50.
f$f f$f f$f Buy the jalopy for $400, not for $475.
My bill is $446. My check is for $442. I owe $4.
The diamond costs $450; the pearl, $40; send $490.

$
4

3. **New-Key Practice: ' (Apostrophe)**

Use apostrophe to indicate:
1. Ownership
2. Contraction
3. Feet

A. The **'** is beside the **;**-key. Use the **;**-finger. Practice the reach from **;** to **'** and back home to **;**. Keep the **J**-finger at home. When you can reach the **'** without looking at your fingers, type this drill twice:

' ' ' ;'; ;'; ;'; It is Kip's job to fix Hap's car.

"
'

Most typewriters have a special !-key. If yours does not, type a period; backspace and type an apostrophe.

B. Type each line twice:

Hello Suzy: Max saw Vicki's car in Jack's garage.
Ben couldn't wear Frank's hat; it wasn't his size.
Dixie is 4 3/4' tall; her brother Quill is 5 1/2'.
Don't pay $9 for the pin! It isn't worth so much!
Marvin, you've done a good job! I'm proud of you!

No space before or after an apostrophe within a word.

LESSON 32
COMPUTER LANGUAGES

Programming languages come in many forms and serve a variety of purposes. The following are just a few computer languages commonly used in business and industry.

BASIC   (Beginners' All-purpose Symbolic Instruction Code) A high-level language consisting of numeric and alphabetic capabilities. It's an interactive means of communication and is used in systems having data communication capabilities.

COBOL   (COmmon Business Oriented Language) The self-documenting language that uses the vocabulary of the business world. It can process numeric and alphabetic information.

RPG II   (Report Program Generator) A problem-oriented language used to generate business reports.

Assembly   Assembly language programs are translated into machine code by a program called assembler. It lets you "talk" to the computer in its native language.

C   Developed by Bell Laboratories as a compiler language. It's noted for its ability to handle conditions that normally would have been written in Assembly language. It contains 32 keywords and is the language in which UNIX was written.

LISP   (LISt Program) Designed for manipulating symbols and for handling strings of information called "lists." It's used in mathematical research and in artificial intelligence.

The Importance of Accuracy

When preparing a computer program, it's imperative that you keyboard accurately, and pay very close attention to spelling and punctuation. The slightest spelling error can cause the program to end with an error message. If you make an error in the placement of a decimal point or you add an extra zero, it will be equivalent to entering the incorrect amount of a check in your checkbook—you get the wrong results. Computers operate by "commands," whose spelling is very specific. Many commands include signs and symbols not normally seen in "human" communication, but they are critical to the proper operation of the program. Needless to say, spelling-checker software in a word processor will be of no use, since the commands are in the language of the computer.

An example of each of the computer languages listed above appears on the following pages. Type each one exactly as it appears, checking very carefully for spelling and accuracy.

4. **Paragraph Practice:** Double Spacing.
   Try for a PERFECT copy of each paragraph.

WORDS

Here is what it cost us to put our men on the   10

moon: $1.1 billion for research; $3.3 billion for   20

designing; $9.4 billion for Saturn Rocket Engines;   30

$7.8 billion for spacecraft; and $2.25 billion for   40

salaries to scientists, office supplies, and help.   50

Total cost of the moon flight: about $24 billion.   60

    1   2   3   4   5   6   7   8   9   10

WORDS

Christopher must catch the bus at 7:30 sharp.   10

He attends St. Michael's School at 47 Bonnie Brown   20

Avenue. He rides the bus with Chrissy and Willie.   30

To succeed you must work hard at what you do.   40

When the going gets rough, breathe deep and go on.   50

Pick yourself up, think of a good thing, be happy.   60

    1   2   3   4   5   6   7   8   9   10

5. **Test Your Skill:** Take Three 3-Minute Timings.
   Goal: 20 words a minute within 4 errors.
           Record your best speed within 4 errors.

WORDS

Your typewriter has some kind of marker known   10

as the printing—point indicator. It points to the   20

space on the scale at which the carriage is set to   30

type the next letter. If the marker points to 50,   40

for example, the carriage is at the 50th space; so   50

the next key you hit will print in the 51st space.   60

    1   2   3   4   5   6   7   8   9   10

4.   Test your skill. Center vertically and horizontally Jobs 2, 3, 4, and 5, each on a half sheet.

Job 2

FREQUENT LEGAL TERMS

Affidavit
Bankruptcy
Complaint
Eviction
Judgment
Plaintiff
Subpoena
Trespass

Job 3

HIGH SCHOOL SUBJECTS

Algebra
Biology
Chemistry
Commercial Law
English
French
Geometry
Italian
Physics
Spanish

Job 4

FAMOUS AMERICAN EXPLORERS

Roy Andrews
Robert Bartlett
Hiram Bingham
Daniel Boone
Richard Byrd
Kit Carson
William Clark
Frederick Cook
Lincoln Ellsworth
John Fremont
Meriwether Lewis
Robert Peary

Job 5

PRINCIPAL BUSINESS JOBS

Bank Teller
Bookkeeper
Cashier

Order Clerk
Shipping Clerk
Payroll Clerk

Office Manager
Receptionist
Salesperson

Stenographer
Telephone Operator
Typist

One blank line between groups.

LESSON 23

(Number or Pounds)
& (Ampersand)

1. **Review:** Type each line twice. Double space after each 2-line group.

Alphabet: `Jack Boxer packed my sledge with five dozen quail.`   Eyes on
All Numbers/$: `f4f  f4$  f$f  The toys are $4.59, $6.75, $8.20, $13.`   copy. Be a
': `k8k  k8k  k'k  k'k  This is Dick's or Luigi's sweater.`   touch
`'  '  '  ;';  ;';  ;';  This is Hap's jalopy, not Kip's.`   typist.
Speedup: `When you take a job, your duty is to do good work.`

        1   2   3   4   5   6   7   8   9   10

2. **New-Key Practice:**   **#** The **#** is on the **3**-key. *Use D-Finger.*
Practice the reach like this: (1) Depress right shift key; (2) Reach for the **3**-key; (3) Move fingers back home. When you can do these 3 steps without looking at your fingers, type each line twice:

No space
between the
sign # and
a number.

`# # # d#d d#d d#d Ship Orders #30, #35, #37, #383.`
`d#d d#d d#d Pay Bills #3, #31, #32, #36, #38, #39.`
`Pack these in lots of 10#, 29#, 38#, 56#, and 74#.`
`d3d d3# d#d d#d The sign # means number or pounds.`
`We shipped 13# of #310 and 53# of #37 to the firm.`

#
3

3. **New-Key Practice:**   **&** The **&** is on the **7**-key. *Use J-Finger.*
Practice the reach like this: (1) Depress the left shift key; (2) Reach for the **7**-key; (3) Move fingers back home. When you can do these 3 steps without looking at your fingers, type each line twice:

One space
before and
after the
sign &.
Type policy
numbers,
order
numbers,
invoice
numbers,
without
commas.

`& & & j&j j&j j&j Sax & Co., Vim & Zale, Mac & Co.`
`j&j j&j j&j Call Fox & Co., Gay & Co., Poe & Bond.`
`Ship at once Webb & Zorn's Order #350 for $492.68.`
`Mail invoices to Lux & Son, Quin & Co., Tyle & Co.`
`Joe's Policy #293648 was issued by Wexler & Smith.`

&
7

Job 1 (Tryout)

FAMOUS EDUCATORS

Socrates
Plato
Aristotle
Martin Luther
Francis Bacon
John Locke
Jean Jacques Rousseau
Friedrich Froebel
Herbert Spencer
Horace Mann
John Dewey

Let us plan and type the above listing.

> Move the margin stops to the extreme ends; clear all tab stops; set line-space regulator at 1; see that the paper guide is at 0; insert a half sheet; center the carriage.

Step 1 is: **To Center the Listing Vertically**

Follow these steps exactly:
1. Jot down the number of lines available on a half sheet 33
2. Jot down the number of lines used in the listing: (12 typed and 2 blank) .... <u>14</u>
3. Jot down the number of lines left over 19
4. Divide the number of lines left over by 2 (for top and bottom margins) 9½
5. Drop the fraction. From top edge of the paper, space down to line 9

Step 2 is: **To Center the Listing Horizontally**

Follow these steps exactly:
1. From the center of the paper, backspace once for every 2 strokes in the heading. The backspacing pairs are:
FA/MO/US/spaceE/DU/CA/TO/RS/ Then type the heading.
2. Space down 3 times to leave 2 blank lines below the heading. Then set the carriage at the center of the paper.
3. Select the longest entry in the listing: Jean Jacques Rousseau
Then backspace once for every 2 strokes. The backspacing pairs are:
Je/an/spaceJ/ac/qu/es/spaceR/ou/ss/ea/ Drop the u.
4. Set the left margin stop when you finish backspacing. The column begins at that point.
5. Type the listing.

4. **Paragraph Practice:** Double Spacing.
   Try for a PERFECT copy of each paragraph:

WORDS

The symbol # typed before a figure stands for   10

the word number. When it is typed after a figure,   20

it stands for the word pounds. This symbol may be   30

used in technical work and in preparing invoices.   40

   1   2   3   4   5   6   7   8   9   10

The symbol & is used only when it is part of   10

the name of a firm. It is correct to write A & P,   20

A & S, Peck & Peck because these firms spell their   30

names this way. But to write Joel & Maxie is poor   40

style unless the reference is to such a firm name.   50

   1   2   3   4   5   6   7   8   9   10

5. **Test Your Skill:** Take Three 3-Minute Timings.
   Goal: 20 words a minute within 4 errors.
   Record your best speed within 4 errors.

WORDS

Use double
spacing.

You may have heard it said that Rome was not   10
built in a day. This means, of course, that time   20
and good effort are needed to turn out good work.   30
The idea holds true with your aim to reach a   40
high skill in what you type. To reach this level   50
takes time and good effort. It's the surest way.   60

   1   2   3   4   5   6   7   8   9   10

LESSON 31
ONE-COLUMN LISTINGS

1. **Review:** Type each line twice. Double space after each 2-line group.

Alphabet:	Hy Maquel rejected five dozen woody packing boxes.
: (Colon):	: : : ;;; ;:; ;:; Dear Kay: Dear Cora: Dear Wally:
Y:	you yam yes; yap yew yet; yen yip yak; yea yah yow
Z:	zero zone zinc; zest zoom zombi; zebra zonal zippy
Speedup:	Six city boys may come here to get work on a farm.

Use a sharp bounce-off tap on the space bar.

1   2   3   4   5   6   7   8   9   10

2. **Test Your Skill:** Take Three 5-Minute Timings.
   Goal: 25 words a minute within 5 errors.
   Record your best speed within 5 errors.

WORDS

Use double spacing.

	WORDS
Every once in a while it is good to check up	10
on your typing technique. Be sure that your pos-	20
ture in front of the machine is correct. Correct	30
posture will help you better your typing skill at	40
a faster rate. Keep your feet flat on the floor.	50
Sit erect as tall as you can and at perfect ease.	60
The chair should be the right height so that your	70
arms slant with your keyboard. Keep elbows close	80
to your body; keep them quiet; let the fingers do	90
the work. Keep eyes on the copy all the time and	100
return the carriage without looking up. All this	110
sums up the rules by which to develop your skill.	120

1   2   3   4   5   6   7   8   9   10

3. **One-Column Listing:**
   A. Material typed in one column is a listing; when typed in 2 or more columns, it is a tabulation.
   B. Always center a listing horizontally. If it is typed on a half or full sheet without other matter, center it vertically and horizontally.
   C. Always type the heading in all CAPITALS. Leave 2 blank lines between the heading and column, starting on the third line below the heading.

LESSON 24
NEW KEYS
% (Percent)   ( ) (Parentheses)

COMPUTER MARGINS: 1" (left and right)
TYPEWRITER MARGINS: 15–70 (Pica)
                       25–80 (Elite)
SPACING: Single

1. **Review:** Type each line twice. Double space after each 2-line group.

Alphabet:	Ray Fan Ted Hig Wes Vic Bob Max Pol Quen Jack Zoel
#:	d3d d3d d#d did Ship 3# of #31 and 73# of #39 now.
P:	pit pat put; pun pew pen; pad pub pot; paw pay pig
Q:	aqua quay quit quip; quiz quest; quiet quail quart
Speedup:	You can make good on any job if you have the urge.

Stretch shift-key finger. Keep other fingers in typing position.

          1   2   3   4   5   6   7   8   9   10

2. **New-Key Practice: %** The % is on the 5-key. *Use F-Finger.*
   (1) Depress right shift key; (2) Reach for the **5**-key; (3) Move fingers back home. Practice these steps till you can do them smoothly—without looking at your fingers. Then type each line twice:

No space between a number and the sign %.

```
% % % f%f f%f f%f Pay 5%; Pay 6%; Pay 7%; Pay 10%;
f%f f%f f%f Tax of 2%, 3%, 4%, 5%, 6%, 7%, 8%, 9%;
f%f f%f f%f Get 5% or 6% interest on the $75 bond.
Max got 10%; Vic got 15%; Zoel got 25%; I got 50%.
Our 5½% rate on the $2,960 note is reduced to 4½%.
```

Keep elbows close to body.

3. **New-Key Practice: ( ) Left and Right Parentheses**
   A. The left parenthesis is on the **9**-key. Use **L**-Finger. (1) Depress left shift key; (2) Reach for **9**-key; (3) Move finger back home. When you can do these steps without looking at your fingers, type this drill twice:

```
191 l(l 191 l(l 191 l(l 191 l(l 191 l(l 191 l(l
```

   B. The right parenthesis is on the **0**-key. Use **;**-Finger. (1) Depress left shift key; (2) Reach for **0**-key; (3) Move finger back home. When you can do these steps without looking at your fingers, type this drill twice:

```
;0; ;); ;0; ;); ;0; ;); ;0; ;); ;0; ;); ;0; ;);
```

   C. Now test your control. Type each line twice; keep elbows close to body.

```
( ( ( l(l l(l l(l The ( is the shift of the 9-key.
) ) ) ;); ;); ;); The ) is the shift of the 0-key.
One (1); Two (2); Three (3); Seven (7); Eight (8);
The reference (the one on page 94) must be quoted.
July 4 is America's Independence Day (since 1776).
```

No space between parentheses and material within them.

1. **Memorandum-Skill Test:** Here are two memoranda. See whether you can arrange them attractively using any of the headings shown.

Memorandum 1

To: All Accounting Personnel/ From: Ethel Maxwell, Supervisor/
Date: *Today's*/ Subject: Computation of Commissions/ I would
like all of you to please compute the new commissions for our
sales personnel inasmuch as the fiscal year will be drawing to
a close.

This is to receive priority attention./ *Your initials*

Memorandum 2

To: All Sales Representatives / From: David
Dworkin, President / Date: Today's /
Subject: Sporting Event Tickets

For many years we have been dis-
tributing tickets to major sporting
events as a Public Relations gesture
to many of our leading clients.

Do you feel the business this is
generating warrants the expense?

XX

4. **Paragraph Practice:** Double Spacing.
   Try for a PERFECT copy of each paragraph:

Did you know that in 1965 American women held	10
70% of all national wealth; 80% of all life insur-	20
ance benefits; 65% of all savings accounts; 48% of	30
all railroad stock; and about 23% of all the jobs?	40

All the
numbers
plus the
new keys.

```
1    2    3    4    5    6    7    8    9    10
```

Independence Day in the United States is July	10
4 (since 1776). July 4 is Independence Day too in	20
the Philippines (since 1946), and Venezuela (since	30
1821). In Argentina it is on July 9 (since 1810).	40

```
1    2    3    4    5    6    7    8    9    10
```

5. **Test Your Skill:** Take Three 3-Minute Timings.
   Goal: 20 words a minute within 4 errors.
   Record your best speed within 4 errors.

All typing beginners make errors. You are no	10
exception. So do not get the feeling that you are	20
clumsy with your hands any time you strike one key	30
for another. Just shrug off those errors you make	40
and keep going. Typing is a skill that takes much	50
practice to learn. You and your friends can learn	60
to type by touch. One only needs a zest to learn.	70

Use double
spacing.

```
1    2    3    4    5    6    7    8    9    10
```

MEMORANDA

The prime objective of the memorandum is to send ideas, decisions, and suggestions to other members of your organization. The memorandum can be sent on a half or full sheet of paper, depending on the length of the message. If your organization uses memoranda frequently, there will probably be a printed letterhead for memoranda.

1. The body of the memorandum starts three lines from the letterhead. If there is no printed letterhead, type the word MEMORANDUM across the center top portion of the paper.

2. Any of the following headings may be used:

    ```
    To:              TO:        TO:

    From:            FROM:      FROM:

    Date:            DATE:      DATE:

    Subject:         SUBJECT:   SUBJECT:
    ```

3. The left margin should align with the typewritten portion of the heading, and the right margin should equal that of the left.

4. The paragraphs should be single spaced, with double spacing between the paragraphs.

```
                    M E M O R A N D U M


        TO:  The Executive Board

      FROM:  Thomas N. Sherrill, President

      DATE:  September 22, 19--

   SUBJECT:  New Insurance Program


             Please be advised that there will be a brief
             meeting on Friday, September 29, 19--, to
             discuss a proposed insurance program.

             All are expected to attend.

             sll
```

LESSON 25

" (Quotation Mark)
__ (Underscore)

COMPUTER MARGINS: 1" (left and right)
TYPEWRITER MARGINS: 15–70 (Pica)
25–80 (Elite)
SPACING: Single

1. **Review:** Type each line twice. Double space after each 2-line group.

```
Alphabet:  frfvb jujmn ftfg jyjh dedc kik, swsx lol. aqaz ;p/     Line 4
     &:    & & j&j j&j Levy & Co., Dix & Son., Smith & Marlon     One space
     %:    f5f f5f f%f f%f I got 15%; Sam, 25%; and Cal, 60%.     between a
     /:    ;/; ;/; ;/; 1/3, 3/4, 10 7/8, 1/9, 14 2/5, 36 2/7.    whole
Speedup:   The old man said the work is too hard for one man.    number and
           1    2    3    4    5    6    7    8    9    10         a "made"
                                                                  fraction.
```

2. **New-Key Practice: " (Quotation Mark)**

   A. The " is on the '-key. Use the left shift key and the ;-finger. Practice the reach: (1) Depress the left shift key; (2) Reach for the apostrophe-key; (3) Move fingers back home. When you can do it smoothly without looking at your fingers, type this drill twice:

   ```
   " " "  ;";  ;";  ;";  Walt said, "Pat can draw a map."
   ```

   Use quotation marks to indicate: quoted material; some titles; seconds; and inches. An apostrophe shows possession and is used to denote minutes and feet.

   B. Type each line twice, double spacing after each 2-line group.

   ```
   "Well," Ben asked, "will you introduce me to her?"      No space
   The teacher said, "Sit erect--as tall as you can."      between
   Cal said he likes the rhythm in Poe's "The Raven."      quotation
   Jim Ryun from Kansas ran an indoor mile in 3' 57".      marks and
   The pugilist was knocked out in 2' 10" of Round 8.      material
                                                           quoted.
   ```

3. **New-Key Practice: __ (Underscore)**

   A. The __ is on the hyphen-key. Use ;-finger. (1) Depress left shift key; (2) Reach for the hyphen-key; (3) Move fingers back home. Practice these steps until you can do them smoothly without looking at your fingers. Then type this drill twice:

   To underscore, move back to first letter; then tap underscore key once for each stroke.

   ```
   __ __ __  ;__;  ;__;  ;__;  Paul Marx is an accurate typist.
   ```

   B. Type each line twice.

   ```
   Rule to remember:  Space twice after typing colon.
   Promises make friends, but performances keep them.
   Five most encouraging words:  "I am proud of you."
   Remember:  Quitters never win; winners never quit.
   ```

   NOTE: If you are using a computer and want to underscore text, check your user manual for instructions for your software.

Address on Letter and Envelope	Salutation and Complimentary Close
(18) *Mayor* Honorable (full name) Mayor of (City) City, State, Zip Code	Dear Mayor (last name): Sincerely yours,
(19) *President of a College or University* President (full name) Name of Institution City, State, Zip Code	Dear President (last name): Sincerely yours,
(20) *Professor at a College or University* Professor (full name) Name of Institution City, State, Zip Code	Dear Professor (last name): Sincerely yours,
(21) *Protestant Clergyman* Reverend (full name) Street City, State, Zip Code	Dear Reverend (last name): Sincerely yours,
(22) *Roman Catholic Priest* Reverend (full name) Street City, State, Zip Code	Dear Reverend Father: Sincerely yours,
(23) *Rabbi* Rabbi (full name) Street City, State, Zip Code	Dear Rabbi: Sincerely yours,
(24) *General, U. S. Army* General (full name) Address of Station	Dear General (last name): Sincerely yours,
(25) *Captain, U. S. Navy* Captain (full name) Address of Station	Dear Captain (last name): Sincerely yours,

4. **Paragraph Practice:** Double Spacing.
Try for 2 PERFECT copies of this paragraph:

WORDS

Use double spacing.

	WORDS
The <u>Americans</u> characterize speech that is not	10
entirely clear by saying "That's Greek to me"; the	20
<u>Russians and Roumanians</u> by "That's Chinese to me";	30
the <u>French</u> by "That's Hebrew to me"; and the <u>Poles</u>	40
by "That's Turkish to me." All have the same idea.	50

```
1     2     3     4     5     6     7     8     9     10
```

5. **Test Your Skill:** Take Three 3-Minute Timings.
Goal: 20 words a minute within 4 errors.
Record your best speed within 4 errors.

WORDS

Use double spacing.

	WORDS
Courage is the nerve to last a trifle longer.	10
John quit his job and applied for a new one there.	20
Fortune smiles on the few--and laughs at the many.	30
A grudge is too heavy a load for anybody to carry.	40
To be calm under stress is the true sign of power.	50
Things will come your way--when you go after them.	60
Ideas must work or they are no better than dreams.	70

```
1     2     3     4     5     6     7     8     9     10
```

Address on Letter and Envelope	Salutation and Complimentary Close
(9) *Representative* Honorable (full name) House of Representatives Washington, D. C. 20515	Dear Mr. (last name): Sincerely yours,
(10) *Librarian of Congress* Honorable (full name) Librarian of Congress Washington, D. C. 20540	Dear Mr. (last name): Sincerely yours,
(11) *Comptroller General* Honorable (full name) The Comptroller General of the United States Washington, D. C. 20548	Dear Mr. (last name): Sincerely yours,
(12) *The Chief of Justice* The Chief Justice The Supreme Court Washington, D. C. 20543	Dear Madam Chief Justice: Sincerely yours,
(13) *Associate Justice* Mr. Justice (last name) The Supreme Court Washington, D. C. 20543	Dear Mr. Justice: Sincerely yours,
(14) *Judge of a Court* Honorable (full name) Judge of the (name of court) Street City, State, Zip Code	Dear Judge (last name): Sincerely yours,
(15) *Clerk of a Court* Mr. (full name) Clerk of the (name of court) Street City, State, Zip Code	Dear Mr. (last name): Sincerely yours.
(16) *Governor of a State* Honorable (full name) Governor of (State) City, State, Zip Code	Dear Governor (last name): Sincerely yours,
(17) *Secretary of State* (of a State) Honorable (full name) Secretary of State of (State) City, State, Zip Code	Dear Mr. Secretary: Sincerely yours,

LESSON 26
NEW KEYS
@ (At)   ¼ (One-Quarter)
* (Asterisk)

COMPUTER MARGINS: 1" (left and right)
TYPEWRITER MARGINS: 15–70 (Pica)
25–80 (Elite)
SPACING: Single

1. **Review:** Type each line twice. Double space after each 2-line group.

Alphabet: Jacquel W. Parky did give them five boxes of zinc.
( ): 191 1(1 ;0; ;); (one) (two) (three) (four) (seven)
" " " " s"s s"s s"s Gwen said, "Show me how to sew."
" " " ;"; ;"; ;"; Walt said, "Pat can draw a map."
Speedup: Last year all the work was done just at this time.

Reach for
all top-row
keys
without
looking up.

   1   2   3   4   5   6   7   8   9   10

2. **New-Key Practice:** @   **(At)**

One space
before and
after the
sign @.

A. @ is on the **2**-key. Use right shift key and **S**-finger. Practice the reach: (1) Depress right shift key; (2) Reach for the **2**-key; (3) Move fingers back home. When you can do these steps without looking at your fingers, type this drill twice:

@ @ @ s@s s@s s@s Get 90 @ 2¢; 62 @ 20¢; 72 @ 21¢.

@
2

B. Type each line twice:

The symbol @ means <u>at</u> or <u>per</u>; as 150 dozen @ 97½¢.
Ship 12 gross (1928) @ $80.65 (less 3½% discount).
Buy 10 @ 56¢; 125 @ 28¢; 374 @ 39¢; and 905 @ 68¢.
Send us 12 boxes @ 59¢ and another 12 boxes @ 60¢.
Try to ship 10 @ 16¢, 28 @ 47¢, and 30 @ 59¢ each.

3. **New-Key Practice:** ¼ *Use ;-Finger.*
The ¼ is on the ½-key. (1) Depress left shift key; (2) Reach for the ½-key; (3) Move fingers back home. Practice these steps until you can do them smoothly without looking at your fingers. Then type each line twice:

No space
between a
number and
the sign ¼.

¼ ¼ ¼ ;¼; ;¼; ;¼; ¼ hour; ¼ week; ¼ month; ¼ year;
For fraction ¼, hold left shift and hit the ½-key.
8 @ 1¼¢ is 10¢; 20 @ 2¼¢ is 45¢; 25 @ 3¼¢ is 81¼¢.
Order 10 more of size 29¼ and 50 more of size 39¼.
Yes, 12 is ¼ of 48; 16 is ¼ of 64; 30 is ¼ of 120.

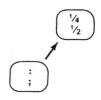

NOTE: As mentioned in Lesson 21, most computers do not have special ½ or ¼ keys; fractions are keyboarded as 1/2, 1/4, or 5/12 on a computer.

SPECIAL FORMS OF ADDRESS, SALUTATION, AND COMPLIMENTARY CLOSE

Special forms of address, salutation, and complimentary close are used for people in high official positions and in special professions. The following forms are commonly used in addressing government officials, educators, clergy, and members of the armed forces:

Address on Letter and Envelope	Salutation and Complimentary Close
(1) *The President* The President The White House Washington, D. C. 20500	Dear Mr. President: Respectfully yours,
(2) *The Vice President* The Vice President United States Senate Washington, D. C. 20510	Dear Mr. Vice President: Sincerely yours,
(3) *Member of Cabinet* The Honorable (full name) The Secretary of (Dept.) Washington, D. C. 20511	Dear Mr. Secretary: Dear Madam Secretary: Sincerely yours,
(4) *Postmaster General* The Honorable (full name) The Postmaster General Washington, D. C. 20260	Dear Mr. Postmaster General: Sincerely yours,
(5) *The Attorney General* The Honorable (full name) The Attorney General Washington, D. C. 20530	Dear Mr. Attorney General: Sincerely yours,
(6) *American Ambassador* The Honorable (full name) American Ambassador City, Country	Sir: Very truly yours,
(7) *United States Senator* Honorable (full name) United States Senate Washington, D. C. 20510	Dear Senator (last name): Sincerely yours,
(8) *Speaker of the House of Representatives* Honorable (full name) Speaker of the House of Representatives Washington, D. C. 20510	Dear Mr. Speaker: Sincerely yours,

4. **New-Key Practice:** * (Asterisk)

The asterisk may be put before or after a word.

A. The * is on the **8**-key. Use **K**-finger. (1) Depress left shift key; (2) Reach for **8**-key; (3) Move fingers back home. Practice these steps until you can do them smoothly without looking at your fingers. Then type this drill twice:

```
* * * k*k k*k k*k Use the asterisk* for footnotes.
```

B. Type each line twice. Double space after each 2-line group.

```
This symbol * is the shift of hyphen or the 8-key.    All the
Special items are marked with the *; as, 50*, 68*.    alphabet
The * directs you to extra text at bottom of page.    keys.
Jackie used the symbol * quite often in her essay.
When Prof. Broz* arrived, I requested him to wait.
```

5. **Paragraph Practice:** Double Spacing.
Try for a PERFECT copy of each paragraph:

WORDS

Use double spacing.

```
     A Roman story tells of a tutor and his pupil,     10
a very young Prince.  The lesson was in Roman His-     20
tory and the Prince was unprepared.  "Now, we come     30
to the Emperor Caligula,*" said the tutor.  "Do you    40
know anything about him, Prince?"  He didn't know.     50
     1    2    3    4    5    6    7    8    9    10

     The tutor's question brought no response from     10
the Prince.  The silence was getting embarrassing,     20
when it was broken by the tactful tutor, who said:     30
"Your Highness is right--perfectly right.  For the     40
less said about the Emperor Caligula, the better."     50
     1    2    3    4    5    6    7    8    9    10

*A very cruel Roman Emperor born A. D. 12,
and assassinated by conspirators A. D. 41.
```

FOLDING AND INSERTING A LETTER

For a Small Envelope: 3 Folds

1. Bring the bottom edge up to about ¼ inch from the top edge and crease.

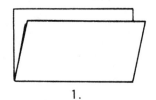

1.

2. Bring the right edge toward the left about ⅓ the width of the paper and crease.

3. Bring the left edge almost to the last fold and crease.

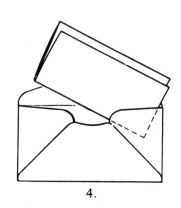

2.   3.

4. Insert the folded letter:
    (a) Hold the envelope with reverse side facing you.
    (b) Insert the letter, last crease first.

For a Large Envelope: 2 Folds

1. Bring bottom edge up to ⅓ the length of the paper and crease.

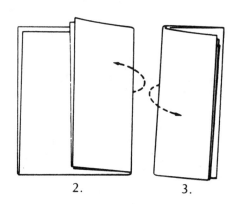

2. Bring top edge down to almost the first crease, leaving a margin of about ¼ inch, and crease.

3. Insert the folded letter:
    (a) Hold the envelope with reverse side facing you.
    (b) Insert the letter, last crease first.

4.

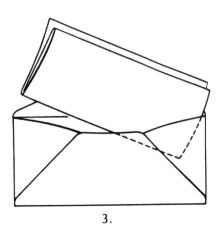

3.

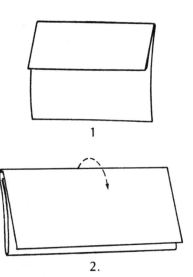

1

2.

6. **Test Your Skill:** Take Three 4-Minute Timings.

Follow these steps in all your 4-minute timings.

A. Repeat if you finish before end of 4 minutes.
B. After each timing, jot down total words typed and total errors.
   Practice the words that have errors till they are easy for you.
C. Your 4-minute speed is words typed divided by 4.
D. Record on your Progress Chart (page 153) your best speed within 4 errors.
   Goal: 22 words a minute within 4 errors.

WORDS

Some people do not practice what they preach;	10
they just do not have more time left for practice.	20
Thrift is doing without something you want so	30
that one day you can buy something you don't need.	40
It's no wonder that King Solomon was so wise:	50
he had 500 wives whom he consulted when uncertain.	60
Doctors tell us that exercise is good for us;	70
so why does it make us feel so tired when we stop?	80
Science can now pinpoint all of our problems;	90
but the only trouble is that it cannot solve them.	100

Double spacing.

1   2   3   4   5   6   7   8   9   10

Lesson 26: @ (At) ¼ * (Asterisk)

"Chainfeeding" Envelopes

"Chainfeeding" is a procedure that enables you to address a large number of envelopes quickly.

1. Set the left margin stop at the desired point for the left margin of the address.

2. Insert envelope to typing position; then put a second envelope behind the cylinder.

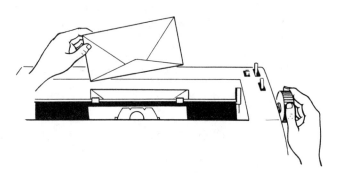

3. Type the first envelope. Twirling it out draws the second one in; insert a third envelope behind the second. Twirling out the second envelope draws the third one in.

4. Continue the "chain." Have an envelope in back of the cylinder while you type the one in the machine.

Suggestion:

Learn to place the address by estimate—like business typists do. Note the amount of space to be left above the address. Practice twirling the envelope into the machine without counting the lines from the top edge.

NOTE: If you need "chainfeeding" capability and are using a computer, you can purchase envelopes that are affixed to continuous paper.

Typing Postal Cards

```
                        (1) August 10, 19—

(2) Dear Madam:

    The TV set which you left with us for
(3) repair is now ready for use.  We have checked (5)
    every part with extreme care and assure you
(4) that it will now give perfect service.

    Please inform us when you will be at home to
    accept delivery.  The full charge is $123.75.

                        Sincerely yours,  (6)

                        APPLIANCE REPAIRS, INC. (7)
```

1. Date: On line 3 from top; start at about the center.
2. Salutation: On line 2 below the date.
3. Spacing: Single; one blank line between paragraphs.
4. Style: Block.
5. Margins: About ½ inch on each side.
6. Complimentary Close: On line 2 below last paragraph; start at about the center.
7. Firm Name: In CAPITALS, on line 2 below complimentary close.

   NOTE: Reference initials may be omitted.

LESSON 27
PERSONAL LETTERS
FULL BLOCK AND
MODIFIED BLOCK STYLES

COMPUTER MARGINS: 1" (left and right)
TYPEWRITER MARGINS: 15–70 (Pica)
25–80 (Elite)
SPACING: Single

1. **Review:** Type each line twice. Double space after each 2-line group.

Alphabet: `abc cde efg ghi ijk klm mno opq qrs stu uvwx xyzab`
R: `raw rap rut; rug rub rob; rid run rip; red ray row`
Underscore: `j__j j__j j__j We must wear a tuxedo at the ceremony.`
`;__; ;__; ;__; I must submit my book report tomorrow.`
Speedup: `To get more pay for the work, you must do it well.`
`1    2    3    4    5    6    7    8    9    10`

Keep hands and arms quiet; let the fingers do the work.

2. **Test Your Skill:** Take Three 4-Minute Timings.
Goal: 22 words a minute within 4 errors.
Record your best speed within 4 errors.

WORDS

Double Spacing.

```
        It is now time to use your skill in the typ-      10

ing of the personal letter.  This is the kind you         20

send to your family and friends.  It is a casual,         30

simple note.  You write just as you talk to them.         40

        The parts of the personal letter are: return      50

address, salutation, body, closing, and signature.        60

At all times it is best to use white letter paper.        70

        Try to type a neat, clear letter to show you      80

think well of the person to whom you are writing.         90

Study the model on the next page and type a copy.         00
        1    2    3    4    5    6    7    8    9    10
```

State Abbreviations

(All Capitals—Without Period)

Alabama	**AL**	Illinois	**IL**	Montana	**MT**	Puerto Rico	**PR**
Alaska	**AK**	Indiana	**IN**	Nebraska	**NB**	Rhode Island	**RI**
Arizona	**AZ**	Iowa	**IA**	Nevada	**NV**	South Carolina	**SC**
Arkansas	**AR**	Kansas	**KS**	New Hampshire	**NH**	South Dakota	**SD**
California	**CA**	Kentucky	**KY**	New Jersey	**NJ**	Tennessee	**TN**
Colorado	**CO**	Louisiana	**LA**	New Mexico	**NM**	Texas	**TX**
Connecticut	**CT**	Maine	**ME**	New York	**NY**	Utah	**UT**
Delaware	**DE**	Maryland	**MD**	North Carolina	**NC**	Vermont	**VT**
D. C.	**DC**	Massachusetts	**MA**	North Dakota	**ND**	Virginia	**VA**
Florida	**FL**	Michigan	**MI**	Ohio	**OH**	Washington	**WA**
Georgia	**GA**	Minnesota	**MN**	Oklahoma	**OK**	West Virginia	**WV**
Hawaii	**HI**	Mississippi	**MS**	Oregon	**OR**	Wisconsin	**WI**
Idaho	**ID**	Missouri	**MO**	Pennsylvania	**PA**	Wyoming	**WY**

Practice in Addressing Envelopes and Postal Cards

From typing paper, cut to size: 6 small envelopes; 6 large envelopes; 6 postal cards. To each address below, type a small envelope; then a large envelope; then a postal card. First: Review the directions on page 84.

Jason & Company, Inc. / 472 Elem Avenue / Philadelphia, PA 25409 / (HOLD)
Fenton Tool Works, Inc. / 310 Court Street / Dallas, TX 43621
White Repair Shop, Inc. / Attention: Mr. Sam Paley / 197 Beacon Street / Newark, NJ 31829

Use all cap method.

Minton Brothers, Inc. / 385 Oakley Building / Yonkers, NY 27065 / (SPECIAL DELIVERY)

Acme Film Company / 641 Broadway / Providence, RI 84062
Dr. George Kane / 615 Morton Lane / Portland, OR 75910 / (PERSONAL)

Addressing Very Large Envelopes

To address an envelope too large for your typewriter—

1. Type the address on a label.

2. Paste the label in about the center of the envelope.

   NOTE: If the envelope does not have the return address, type it in the upper left part of the label.

3. **Letter Practice:** In the Full Block style, everything starts at the margin. For mixed punctuation, place a colon after the salutation and a comma after the closing. For open punctuation, omit the colon after the salutation and the comma after the closing. All other punctuation remains the same.

If your machine is Pica, copy Model 1 exactly—line for line. If your machine is Elite, type more words to the line in order to make the side margins come out about equal. Listen for the bell.

Model 1 Short Personal Letter Single Spaced Pica Type Mixed Punctuation	COMPUTER MARGINS: 1" (left and right) TYPEWRITER MARGINS: 15–75 (Pica) 20–85 (Elite) START: 20 lines from top

```
2830 Shore Road
Brooklyn, NY 11220
July 3, 19--



Dear Norma:

Would you like to come along with me and mother on an auto trip
to Bronxville?  We are going to visit my aunt Marilyn.  She
said she would be happy to see you.

If you can go, please put a few things in your suitcase and be
ready by 11 AM, July 7.  We will pick you up in our car.  Tell
mother and dad that we will bring you home before noon on July
10.

Sincerely,
```

(72 Words)

NOTE: A short letter is under 125 words. In such letters, start the salutation approximately on line 20.

ADDRESSING ENVELOPES AND POSTAL CARDS

Standard postal card is 5½ × 3¼ inches.

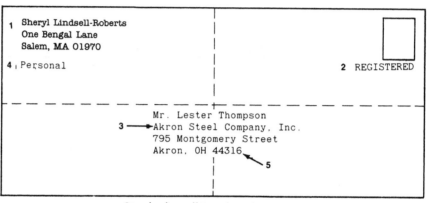

Standard small envelope is 6½ × 3⅝ inches.
Standard large envelope is 9½ × 4⅛ inches.

NOTE: The address typed in all capital letters—without punctuation—conforms to the recommendations of the U.S. Postal Service. (Observe the abbreviations of AVE, ST, BLVD, RD, etc.)

The numbers in the figures are explained below. (The broken lines show the vertical and horizontal centers.)

1. **Return Address:**
    (If not printed)
    Block form, single space. Begin on line 3 from top edge and 3 spaces from left edge.

2. **Postal Notation:**
    Type under the stamp any special postal notations such as REGISTERED, SPECIAL DELIVERY, CERTIFIED, etc.

3. **Mailing Address:**
    Envelopes and Postal Cards
    Block form, single space. Type the name at the estimated vertical center. This would be on line 12 of a small envelope, line 14 of a large envelope, line 10 of a postal card. Start it about ½ inch to the left of the center point.

4. **Special In-House Notations:**
    Type special notations for the company such as Attention, Personal, Please Forward, Hold, etc. under the return address.

5. **Zip Code:**
    Type the Zip Code 1 space after the state. Use the new 2-letter state abbreviations listed on page 85, approved by the U.S. Postal Service.

4. **Letter Practice:** In the Modified Block style, the inside address, date, and complimentary closing start in the center. Set a tab stop in the center of the paper—42 for Pica or 50 for Elite. Everything else remains as in the Full Block style.

If your machine is Pica, copy Model 2 exactly—line for line. If your machine is Elite, type more words to the line to make margins come out about equal. Listen for the bell.

Model 2
Short Personal Letter
Single Spaced
Pica Type
Open Punctuation

COMPUTER MARGINS: 1" (left and right)
TYPEWRITER MARGINS: 15–75 (Pica)
                      20–85 (Elite)
START: 18 lines from top

```
                              275 West 86 Street
                              New York, NY 10024
                              April 17, 19--


Dear Ralph

Dr. William Brown, Director of Civil Defense at the Hudson
Institute, will speak in Townsend Harris Hall, 138 Street and
Amsterdam Avenue, next Thursday evening at 7:30 on the "Hudson
View of Disarmament."  The Hudson Institute makes studies of
our national security.

I am sure that you would like to hear this talk.  Dr. Brown is
a dynamic speaker.  He will have a message of interest to all
City College students.

The lecture will be followed by a discussion period.  It is
sponsored by the City College Chapter of the Universities
Committee on Problems of War and Peace.

If you can make it that evening, phone me at home before 5:30.

                              Sincerely
```

(113 Words)

TWO-PAGE LETTERS

Most business letters require only one page. If a letter is too long for one page:

1. End the first page about one inch from the bottom. Make a light pencil mark 1½ inches from bottom. Type 3 more lines after reaching this mark.

2. End the page with a complete paragraph if you can; if you cannot, leave at least 2 lines and carry over at least 2 lines to page 2.

3. On page 2, line 6 from top edge, type the addressee's name, the page number, and the date. These may be blocked at the left margin or spread evenly across the page. See models below.

4. Continue the letter on line 3 below the page 2 heading. Use the same line length as on page 1.

5. Use plain paper (without letterhead) of the same size and quality as page 1.

Always used for full block.

```
Times Appliance Company, Inc.
Page 2
April 12, 1984


Your instructions will be followed exactly.   Detailed
prices and a total for each part are listed.   We shall
```

Used for all other styles.

```
Mr. Charles H. Andrews      2                June 6, 1984

     If the plans are changed, we shall submit a revised
list to you.  If the plans are not changed, we are ready
```

5. **Letter-Skill Test:** Below is a short unarranged personal letter. Type it 2 times: once in Full Block style, like Model 1; and once in Modified Block style, like Model 2.

Remember: Listen for the bell—it rings when the carriage is 7 or 8 spaces from the right margin. When you hear the bell:
(1) Finish a short word (5 or fewer letters)
or
(2) Divide a long word between syllables. Type a hyphen at the end of the line and finish the word on the next line.

NOTE: If the keys lock and you need only 1 or 2 more spaces to finish the line, press the margin release key at top of keyboard.

```
Your Home Address
Today's Date

Dear Maxie:  Today we learned to type personal letters in the
Full Block and Modified Block styles.

In the Full Block style everything begins at the margin; in the
Modified Block style the inside address, date, and complimen-
tary closing are centered or slightly to the right of center.
Otherwise, both styles are alike.

Next week we learn to type business letters.  As soon as I have
done some of them, I will send you samples.

I am glad to hear that you got the job you were after.  Well, I
hope you are happy now and are doing well.

Sincerely,
```

(79 Words)

2. **Letter-Skill Test:** Here are two average-length, unarranged letters. See whether you can arrange them attractively in any style. Use today's date.

Letter 1

Mr. John Clarkson, Manager/ Boyntex Auto Supplies, Inc./ 240 Madison Boulevard/ Milwaukee, WI 18107 Dear Mr. Clarkson: Within the next few months you may expect to receive requests for information concerning the new tubeless tires that have recently been developed. There will no doubt be a great demand for these tires because their many unusual features afford maximum riding comfort and ease of driving.

We plan to include in our stock a complete line of this superior product. There may be some delay, however, as manufacturers are having difficulty meeting the current demand.

Don't forget to include your initials.

A small shipment that may be used for display purposes should reach you this week. Please inform your customers that we shall do our best to fill their orders promptly./ Sincerely yours,/ HARMON TIRE COMPANY, INC./ George Rice/ Sales Manager

(106 Words)

Letter 2

Mr. William T. Ford/ Federal Insurance Company/ 283 Doyle Drive, Bangor, ME 04401 Dear Mr. Ford: We are very sorry to learn that the public address system we installed two months ago has not been working satisfactorily. We assure you that we will correct this situation at once.

You realize that it is difficult for us to tell you the exact reason for its failure until we make a complete inspection. However, it is quite possible that some of the tubes are defective or that one of the loudspeakers is not in perfect condition.

As you suggested, one of our engineers will phone you next week for an appointment to visit you. At that time, he will make all necessary repairs. Yours truly,/ PUBLIC ADDRESS SYSTEMS, INC./ Henry J. Silver/ Chief Inspector

(105 Words)

LESSON 28
BUSINESS LETTERS
FULL BLOCK AND
MODIFIED BLOCK

COMPUTER MARGINS: 1" (left and right)
TYPEWRITER MARGINS: 15–70 (Pica)
                       25–80 (Elite)
SPACING: Single

1. **Review:** Type each line twice. Double space after each 2-line group.

Alphabet:	wavy list neat axle quip from doze high jury backs
S:	sap sun sit; sir sob sol; sub six sew; say sod sip
@:	s@s s@s s@s Ship 12 @ 16¢; 32 @ 46¢; and 52 @ 56¢.
Speedup:	The boss may put a new man on this job to help us.

Try to type
without
pauses.

          1   2   3   4   5   6   7   8   9   10

2. **Paragraph Practice:** Type the following paragraph for practice.

Double
Spacing.

        A letter that you type to a place of business
is a business letter; it is much like the personal letter that you practiced in the previous
lesson. In personal letters, your return address, the
date, and the closing lines begin at the top of
the paper and are put in blocked form. But in the
business letter, the return address is on the
letterhead and you have to add the name
and address of the business to which you are
writing. This part is known as the inside address.
Study the model on the next page; then type a copy.

LESSON 30
ADDITIONAL LETTERS,
2-PAGE LETTERS, ENVELOPES,
POSTAL CARDS, AND MEMORANDA

COMPUTER MARGINS: 1" (left and right)
TYPEWRITER MARGINS: 12–75 (Pica)
15–90 (Elite)
START: Line 10 or 12

1. **Letter Practice:** Copy Model 1 exactly if your machine is Pica; if it is Elite, type more words to the line to make the side margins come out about equal. Listen for the bell.

On Line 12   October 28, 19--

Start 4 lines
below date.

Model 1
Long Business Letter
Full Block Style
Pica Type

Mr. Joseph Wagner
175 Turnpike Road
Boston, MA 02139

Dear Mr. Wagner:

Do you need extra money again this year?

You know from past experience that if you start selling Christmas Cards early, you make the most money. Your complete set of samples is ready and waiting for you. Again you will have the first opportunity to show your customers the best-designed and value-packed assortment in the greeting card industry.

Our FABULOUS FOILS Christmas Assortment contains 21 of the most beautiful cards you ever saw, and costs your customer only $2. These same 21 cards, if sold separately, cost up to 35 cents a card in any store. So you give your customer a $7.35 value for only $2.00.

You make $1 for selling 1 box; $2 for selling 2 boxes; $10 for selling 10 boxes; $50 for selling 50 boxes, etc., of our FABULOUS FOILS. Everybody buys at least 1 box of Christmas Cards. Many buy 4 and 5 boxes. So you make $1, $2, $3, $4, or more on almost every call. Last year, our records show, you made $102.

Your new sample kit, which we shall send you on approval, contains 4 boxes, all different. You may return them at our expense anytime within 20 days if you don't like them. As before, please send no money. Just fill in the card enclosed and mail it today.

Sincerely,

1 blank line

FABULOUS FOILS, INC.

Norman S. Kelvin
Sales Manager

HC
Enclosure

(220 Words)

SAMPLE BUSINESS LETTER

(1) Date	September 16, 19—
(2) Mailing/In-House Notation	CERTIFIED MAIL
(3) Inside Address	Jon Allan, Inc.
(4) Attention Line	Attn: Eric Laurence 24 Parnassus Way Tallman, NY 10982
(5) Salutation	Gentlemen:
(6) Subject Line	Subject: Ski Show Contract
(7) Body or Message	I am enclosing the contract we agreed upon stipulating all the terms and conditions of the ski show that will take place at the Marc Alan Community College during the week of December 2. Can we meet for lunch on either Wednesday or Thursday of next week in order to finalize arrangements? If neither date is convenient, please call so that we can arrange a mutually convenient time.
(8) Complimentary Closing	Sincerely yours,
(9) Signature Line	Sheryl Lindsell-Roberts
(10) Reference Initials **(11) Enclosure Notation** **(12) Copy Notation**	jt Enclosure pc: Marc Alan Community College
(13) Postscript	The camping show contract will be ready next month.

Sheryl Lindsell-Roberts

117 Sudbury Street, Marlborough, MA 01752 • (508)229-8209

6. **Letter-Skill Test:** Below are two average-length, unarranged letters. See whether you can arrange them attractively. Use today's date.

Letter 1 (Semiblock Style)

Indent all paragraphs 5 spaces.

Mr. James T. Reid/ Acme Realty Company/ 394 Seventh Avenue/ Atlanta, GA 31403/ Dear Mr. Reid: In response to your request, we shall be glad to submit an estimate for installing two elevators in the new apartment house you are building at 286 Park Boulevard. We are happy to have this opportunity to serve you and will mail an itemized bid by the end of next week.

Although our bid may not be the lowest you receive, may we ask that you consider these facts before awarding the contract: We have been in business in this city for over 60 years and manufacture a high-grade product. We enjoy a reputation for excellent workmanship.

Include your initials. Do not include the "P.S." notation in the letter.

If you decide to deal with our concern, we assure you of thorough satisfaction. Yours truly, SWEM & CO., INC. Samuel Hoffman, Chief Engineer/ Furthermore, our one-year guarantee provides complete and regular inspections.

(122 Words)

Letter 2 (Simplified Style)

Bryant Hardware, Inc./ 372 Farragut Street/ Philadelphia, PA 19142/ SUBJECT: LUXOR FANS/ Thank you for your interest in our Luxor Fans. Our representative, Mr. Fred Karlin, has been instructed to call on you within ten days. Mr. Karlin will make a definite appointment by telephone.

Our booklet listed only 60-cycle models because this is the type most commonly ordered. However, we can supply 40-cycle motors in any model without extra charge. Mr. Karlin will discuss this matter with you in detail.

All reports indicate that when hot weather comes there will be a strong demand for the new Luxor Fans with their durable motors and attractive colors. Demand should result in increased profits, and we want you to have your share./ George Flexner, President

(111 Words)

Standard Letter Parts

(1) Date Line: Current date with no abbreviations

(2) Mailing Notations: Special Delivery, Certified Mail, Registered Mail,
                        etc.
    In-House Notations: Confidential, Hold, etc.

(3) Inside Address: Name and address of company or person to whom letter is written

(4) Attention Line: Directly under name of company

(5) Salutation: Must be in accord with first line of inside address ("Gentlemen" to a company,
    "Dear Sir or Madam" to an individual whose name is unknown, or "Dear ----" to an
    individual whose name is known)

(6) Subject Line: Gives reader theme of letter

(7) Body: Single spaced with double spacing between paragraphs

(8) Complimentary Closing: Only first letter capitalized
    Formal   Yours truly, Very truly yours, Yours very truly,
                Respectfully, Respectfully yours,
    Informal Sincerely, Sincerely yours, Cordially, Cordially yours,
    Personal Best wishes, As always, Regards, Kindest regards,

(9) Signature Line: Very truly yours,   Very truly yours,

                                            ABC COMPANY, INC.

                     John Smith

                                            John Smith, President

5. **Letter-Skill Test:** Below is an average-length business letter. Type it 2 times: once in the Semiblock style, like Model 3; and once in the Simplified style, like Model 4.

```
                    L E T T E R H E A D



                         July l7, 19--



Hamilton Bags, Inc.
Attention Mr. Tom Galati
382 North Avenue
Chicago, IL 60609

Gentlemen:

Subject: Order No. 8198

     I am very much disappointed with your service in filling my
order of July 10 for Blue Patent Leather Handbags.

     The package reached me this morning.  When I examined the
bags, I found that they were not the style I ordered.  I speci-
fied Model DX, as advertised in THE TRIBUNE, with no initials
embossed under the snaplock.  You sent Model A, which is entirely
too small for my needs, and some contained initials.

     I am returning the handbags to you today by insured parcel
post and would appreciate it if you would send the correct
handbags promptly.  I am starting my big sale on July 30 and
would like to have the handbags by that time.

     Thank you for your attention to this matter.

                         Sincerely yours,



                         Jane Murphy, Manager

JM/fb
```

(126 Words)

(10) Reference Initials: Initials of typist

(11) Enclosure Notation: When enclosure is being sent with letter (When something is attached, "Attachment" may be used in place)

(12) Copy Notation: When stat copy of letter is being sent to third person ("PC" used for indicating photostatic copy or "BCC" used to send copy when writer does not want to apprise addressee of same. Said notation appears only on the copies—not on the original.)

(13) Postscript: Afterthought or emphasis (do not include "PS" notation)

PLACEMENT OF LETTER

Short Letter	(approximately 125 words or less)
	Computer Margins: 1" (left and right)
	Typewriter Margins: 15 and 75 (Pica)
	20 and 85 (Elite)
	Start: Line 19 or 20

Average Letter	(approximately 126–225 words)
	Computer Margins: 1" (left and right)
	Typewriter Margins: 15 and 75 (Pica)
	15 and 90 (Elite)
	Start: Line 15–18

Long Letter	(approximately 226 words or more)
	Computer Margins: 1" (left and right)
	Typewriter Margins: 12 and 75 (Pica)
	15 and 90 (Elite)
	Start: Line 10 or 12

4. **Letter Practice:** In the Simplified style, the salutation and complimentary closing are omitted. The subject line appears in all capital letters three lines below the inside address and three lines above the body. The writer's name appears four lines below the body, also in all capital letters. All parts of this letter style are blocked; therefore, no tabs need to be set. Type a copy of Model 4.

Model 4
Short Business Letter
Simplified Style
Single Spaced
Pica Type

Margins: 15–75 (Pica)
20–85 (Elite)
Start: 20 lines from top

```
April 20, 19--

Mr. Lester Thompson
Harmon Silk Co., Inc.
376 Montgomery Street
Akron, OH 44316

SUBJECT: BILINGUAL SECRETARIAL POSITION

About two months ago I inquired by letter whether you could use
an experienced bilingual secretary with knowledge of Spanish.
You informed me that you had no openings then but that you
would place my name on file.

Although I am now employed, I am still interested in working
for your Export Division.  You will note, by referring to
my original letter of application, that I have all the
qualifications for the job and that I will make an excellent
secretary.

May I hear from you soon concerning the prospects of my joining
your export staff.


MEREDITH STONE
```

(100 Words)

3. **Letter Practice:** In the Full Block style, everything begins at the margin. Clear the machine. If your machine is Pica, copy Model 1 *exactly*—line for line. If your machine is Elite, type more words to the line in order to have the side margins come out about equal. Listen for the bell.

Model 1
Short Business Letter
Full Block Style
Pica Type
Mixed Punctuation

Start on line
20 at
margin.

February 10, 19--

Start 4 lines
below date.

Mr. O. V. Poole
409 East 35 Drive
Wichita, KS 67202

Dear Mr. Poole:

SUBJECT: ACCOUNT NO. 8198

Your credit reputation is probably your most valuable asset.
Yet you are jeopardizing your credit rating for $79.38, the
balance of your account with us.

Since you have ignored our previous four letters, there seems
to be no alternative for us except to turn this matter over to
our attorneys.

You can make this action unnecessary by mailing your check in
the enclosed stamped envelope.

Yours truly,

1 blank line

STAR GOODS CO., INC.

4 blank
lines

John Doe
Vice-President

JN
Enclosure

(67 Words)

3. **Letter Practice:** In the Semiblock style, paragraphs begin 5 spaces from the left margin. You already have a tab stop for paragraph indentions, which you set for the 4-minute timings. Now, set another tab stop at the center for the date and the closing lines. Type a copy of Model 3.

Model 3
Average-length
Business Letter
Semiblock Style
Pica Type
Mixed Punctuation

Start on line
8 below
date.

December 12, 19--

Allen Screvane & Sons
Attention Eric Laurence
738 Van Alston Avenue
Los Angeles, CA 90017

Gentlemen:

We are enclosing a check for $375 to be credited to our account. We had expected to pay the full amount when the invoice became due, and we regret that we are unable to send you a larger amount at the present time.

You will recall that the shipment of topcoats did not reach us until two weeks after the date on which you promised delivery. This caused a delay in the display of our stock, which resulted in a slowing up of sales. Collections, too, are still poor in this town. Accordingly, we shall be unable to pay the balance of this account before the first of next month.

We hope you will realize the position we are in and grant us this extension.

Sincerely yours,

PERRY BROTHERS, INC.

Warren Bergstein
Credit Manager

DW
Enclosure

(126 Words)

4. **Letter Practice:** Copy Model 2 *exactly* if your machine is Pica; if it is Elite, type more words to the line to make the side margins come out about equal. Listen for the bell.

Model 2
Average-length
Business Letter
Modified Block Style
Pica Type
Open Punctuation

August 2, 19--

Start on line
15 at center

Start 4 lines
below date.

Mrs. Norma Meyers
856 Leonard Street
Newark, NJ 07102

No colon.

Dear Mrs. Meyers

Thank you for your letter of July 27. We are pleased to hear from you and enclose the catalog you desire. It describes in detail the new line of appliances now on display in our local showrooms.

Our stock includes the finest brands with a guarantee for 90 days. For a limited time only, many items are now being offered at greatly reduced prices. There is just a small charge for labor when we make an installation in your home.

If you wish any further details about the equipment we carry, you may call or visit our sales office between the hours of 9 and 5 daily except Sunday. We suggest that you make your choice now in order to benefit from our summer clearance prices.

Cordially yours

DIX APPLIANCE CO., INC.

No comma.

Thomas Benardo
General Manager

RJ
Enclosure

(126 Words)

LESSON 29
BUSINESS LETTERS
SEMIBLOCK AND
SIMPLIFIED STYLES

COMPUTER MARGINS: 1" (left and right)
TYPEWRITER MARGINS: 15–70 (Pica)
                      25–80 (Elite)
SPACING: Single

1. **Review:** Type each line twice. Double space after each 2-line group.

```
Alphabet:  frfvb jujmn ftfg jyjh dedc kik, swsx lol. aqaz ;p/   Depress
       V:  van vow vex vim via vote; vend void vice vase view   shift key
       *:  k8k k8* k*k k*k The asterisk* is a reference mark.    firmly.
 Speedup:  No man who does not do all the work will get paid.
            1     2     3     4     5     6     7     8     9    10
```

2. **Paragraph Practice:** Type the following paragraphs for practice.

```
        You have learned that in the modified block style

business letter all the parts are started from the

left margin, except the date and the closing lines.

You start these lines at the center of your paper.

        The semiblock style letter is almost the

same as the modified block.  The only difference is

that here you have to set two tab stops:  the first,

five spaces from your left margin to indent every

paragraph; the second, at the center of the paper,

for the date and the closing lines.  Take a moment to

study the model on the next page, then type it.
```

5. **Letter-Skill Test:** Following are four short, unarranged letters. See whether you can arrange each on a separate sheet. Listen for the margin bell.

Letter 1 (Full Block Style)

Everything starts at the margin.

Today's Date / The Graphic Magazine/ 725 Clary Street/ Fort Worth, TX 76112/ Gentlemen:/ SUBJECT: CONTRACT NO. 762/ Will you please cancel our advertising contract in your publication to take effect immediately.

Business conditions have compelled us to curtail a considerable portion of our advertising appropriation for the next six months.

Much to our regret, we must eliminate the magazine from our list./ Yours truly,/ MARVIN & MAXWELL, INC./ Jack Samuels/ Advertising Manager/ *Your initials*

(45 Words)

Letter 2 (Full Block Style)

Everything starts at the margin.

Today's Date / Mr. Sidney Harris/ 1756 Leewood Drive/ Hartford, CT 30943/ Dear Mr. Harris:/ Our records show that the bill covering final charges of $27.50 for your gas and electric service has not been paid.

We shall appreciate prompt payment of this bill so that the account may be closed. Payment may be made by mail or in person at any Intercounty Lighting Company office. It is important that you clear up this amount before you move./ Yours sincerely,/ INTERCOUNTY LIGHTING COMPANY/ Vincent Kendall/ Collection Department/ *Your initials*

(63 Words)

Lesson 28: Business Letters—Full and Modified Block

Letter 3 (Modified Block Style)

Start the date and complimentary closing at the center.

Today's Date / McClure & Rider, Inc./ Attention Thomas N. Sherrill/ 920 Madison Avenue/ New York, NY 10028/ Gentlemen:/ May I ask a favor of you?

As secretary of the Advanced Typing Class at Wadleigh Evening High School, in Manhattan, I am collecting a variety of successful sales letters and circulars for display on our business bulletin board.

Because your agency is so well known for its effective advertising, I would appreciate receiving a few of your mail order samples and circulars.

Thank you for whatever material you can furnish./ Sincerely yours,/ Emma Jones/ *Your initials*

(70 Words)

Letter 4 (Modified Block Style)

Start the date and complimentary closing at the center.

Today's Date / The Personnel Department/ ABC Company, Inc./ 607 Smith Hill Road/ Pasadena, CA 91106/ Dear Mr. Hamill:/ Please consider me a candidate for the Receptionist–Typist position advertised in THE NEW YORK TIMES on Sunday. I have an excellent typing background and am skilled at dealing with people.

Although the enclosed resume outlines the details of my background, you will undoubtedly have many questions you would like answered. May I, therefore, have an interview at your convenience?

I would very much like the opportunity to put my skills and talents to work for you./ Very truly yours,/ Janice N. Morton/ *No initials when you sign the letter*

(determine the length)